Effective Sales Forecasting

Steven M. Bragg

AccountingTools®

Table of Contents

About the Author

Steven Bragg, CPA, has been the chief financial officer or controller of four companies, as well as a consulting manager at Ernst & Young. He received a master's degree in finance from Bentley College, an MBA from Babson College, and a Bachelor's degree in Economics from the University of Maine. He has been a two-time president of the Colorado Mountain Club, and is an avid alpine skier, mountain biker, and certified master diver. Mr. Bragg resides in Centennial, Colorado. He has written more than 300 books and courses, including *New Controller Guidebook*, *GAAP Guidebook*, and *Payroll Management*.

Steven maintains the accountingtools.com web site, which contains continuing professional education courses, the Accounting Best Practices podcast, and thousands of articles on accounting subjects.

Buy Additional AccountingTools Courses

AccountingTools offers more than 1,500 hours of CPE courses, with concentrations in accounting, auditing, finance, taxation, and ethics. Related courses that you might like include:

- Budgeting: A Comprehensive Guide
- Capital Budgeting
- Financial Analysis
- Financial Forecasting and Modeling
- Operations Management

Go to accountingtools.com/cpe to view these additional courses.

AccountingTools®

Chapter 1
Essential Elements of Sales Forecasting

Introduction

When performed correctly, sales forecasting can provide substantial benefits for a business. It forms the foundation for the proper allocation of resources throughout an organization. However, when conducted improperly, it can have the reverse effect, potentially causing severe losses. Consequently, the forecaster must have a sound knowledge of the elements of a forecast, the drivers of forecast accuracy, and forecasting techniques – all of which are covered in this chapter.

The Importance of Sales Forecasting

Anyone who has developed a comprehensive budget understands the value of sales forecasting, because many parts of the budget can only be developed by referring back to the forecast. For example, how much production capacity should the firm install? This decision is based entirely on the sales forecast. Similarly, the amount of production staffing to plan for, the amount of finished goods inventory to keep on hand, and the staffing of many departments is primarily based on the sales forecast. Consequently, having a reasonable understanding of the amount of revenue to be expected, as well as its timing, is essential to operational planning.

However, when a sales forecast turns out to be incorrect, the corporate planning function goes badly awry. In this scenario, the company makes either excessively high or low investments in its production capacity, hires too many people or too few, and invests in either too much or too little inventory. In the first case, the firm has been wasteful in investing in its future. In the latter case, the firm is not prepared for a sales surge, and will likely have to forego a certain amount of sales that it might otherwise have secured with better planning. Here are several other costs associated with sales forecasts that do not reflect reality:

- The cost of any products damaged due to unnecessary transport between distribution hubs.
- The loss of margin from selling excess products after the prime selling season.
- The cost of more rapid freight charges to access raw materials in less than the standard time.
- The amount of lost sales due to not having sufficient units in stock.
- The cost of excess production line setups to work around insufficient raw materials on hand.
- The cost of holding excess amounts of inventory.
- The cost of customers lost due to inventory shortfalls.

EXAMPLE

The Twister Vacuum Company makes the most powerful vacuum cleaners in the world. Its overly aggressive sales staff issues a sales forecast for the upcoming year that is 30% higher than for the preceding year. Based on this information, the purchasing department enters into a binding purchase order to acquire custom-molded parts for over 100,000 vacuum cleaners, in exchange for a substantial volume discount. Unfortunately, sales turn out to be flat, so the company has to both pay for and store the extra parts in its warehouse.

EXAMPLE

Billabong Machining Company produces widgets. It has historically had significant difficulty predicting the number of units that will be sold, so it has opted to produce too many widgets, in order to have enough units on hand whenever a customer calls with an order. When conducting a comparison of inventory levels to actual sales, the company's controller estimates that the company has been investing an excess $5 million in inventory per year. Therefore, if the company can improve the accuracy of its sales forecasts by just 20%, it can also reduce its excess inventory by 20%, resulting in a $1 million working capital reduction. In addition, the company might be able to shrink its warehouse space requirements in conjunction with the decline in widget inventory.

EXAMPLE

Active Exercise Machines produces treadmills for the home exercise market. Based on an excessively optimistic sales forecast, the company produces several thousand extra treadmills. To clear out this inventory, it is forced to drop prices by 30%, as well as to spend $10,000 on an on-line ad campaign to notify customers of the special deal. In addition, the massive sale spreads the rumor among customers that Active will now engage in an annual sale, so they all delay their purchases in the following year, in expectation of another discount.

We have referred to the cost of maintaining excess amounts of inventory. Just how much are we talking about? This requires a detailed review of *holding costs*, which are the costs incurred to store inventory. There are a number of different holding costs, including the following:

- *Depreciation.* A business incurs a depreciation charge in each period for all storage space, racks, and equipment that it owns in order to store and handle inventory. This can be a substantial charge if the company has invested large amounts in automated storage and retrieval systems.
- *Insurance.* A firm should have insurance coverage for its inventory asset. If so, the cost of insurance related to this coverage is a holding cost.
- *Obsolete inventory write-offs.* If inventory is held too long, it may no longer be sellable. If so, it is written off as soon as it is designated as obsolete. This can be a substantial cost, especially in businesses where new products appear on a regular basis.

- *Personnel.* The cost of the warehouse staff that relates to storage is a holding cost. Besides compensation, this cost includes employee benefits and payroll taxes.
- *Rental space.* The cost of warehouse rental space is a holding cost, and can be excessive if the storage systems in place do not make complete use of the cubic volume of the facility.
- *Security.* If the inventory is valuable, it makes sense to have security guards, fencing, and monitoring systems in place, all of which are holding costs.

Inventory holding costs can easily be 20% of the total value of inventory, so when an incorrectly-high forecast triggers the purchase of excessive amounts of inventory, remember to add 20% to the cost of the inventory – this is an additional cost of an incorrect forecast.

Problems with Sales Forecasting

How can a sales forecast be so incorrect that it interferes with the operations of a business? In the following sub-sections, we cover some of the more critical issues that may arise.

Flawed Assumptions

The assumptions underlying a forecast may be flawed. For example, the forecasting team may assume that all current customers will continue to buy from the company in the same volumes that it did in the past. Or, management may incorrectly assume that sales volumes will hold up, despite a planned increase in prices. Another questionable assumption is that sales from an existing sales region can be increased, despite no evidence that this is possible. Management could be basing its forecasting on dozens of assumptions like these, some of which may turn out to be true, and some of which will not.

Unreliable Data

The data being used to compile a forecast are unreliable. This can be a problem when historical sales data are aggregated from several subsidiaries, or when the data come from within one entity, but earlier records were stored in a different accounting system (or spreadsheet). It is also possible that earlier sales data were recorded under accounting standards that have since been altered, resulting in data that are not readily comparable. When the data are muddled in this manner, forecasts derived from it are more likely to contain outcomes that differ substantially from actual results.

EXAMPLE

Giro Cabinetry recently acquired a firm that also makes cabinets. In compiling the sales data from both firms to create the annual forecast, Giro's forecasting team fails to notice that the sales data provided by the acquiree does not strip out sales taxes from its sales totals, so that the sales figures are too high by 7%. By using this data, the forecasting team creates a sales forecast for the combined entity that is too high.

Excessively Detailed Forecasts

Management may mandate the creation of excessively detailed forecasting models. The concern here is that a massive amount of time may be spent formulating the exact number of units that will be sold for each stock-keeping unit (SKU) and the exact price points at which they will be sold, when it is not possible to actually do so. In reality, these numbers will vary over time, and especially at a deep level of detail.

Ignorance of Unit Volumes

Forecasts are usually compiled in terms of sales dollars, rather than the underlying number of units. The problem here is that projecting sales dollars can mask important changes in the underlying unit volume data. For example, unit sales may be declining even while projected sales dollars increase, because the company is increasing its price points. This unit volume decline is a serious issue that management should address – except that it may not know, because of the structure of the forecast.

EXAMPLE

Laid Back Corporation sells a variety of business chairs. For the next year, its sales forecast shows a 12% increase in total sales dollars. The company does not forecast the number of units sold. What this situation masks is that total unit volume is actually declining slightly; sales are increasing, because the market has shifted toward the company's more expensive chairs, while overseas competitors are underpricing its lower-cost chairs.

Misunderstanding of the Customer

Another issue is that the company does not really understand who its customers are or why they buy its products, in which case it may be blindsided when these poorly-understood customers suddenly shift away.

EXAMPLE

A major book publisher has never delved into the details of why a few of its customers buy the publisher's accounting books in large volume. It turns out that they are all continuing professional education training companies, and use the books as part of their training materials. However, the rules imposed on them by the National Association of State Boards of Accountancy are changed, so that bound books can no longer be used as training materials. Because of this change, the publisher is completely blindsided by a major drop in its book sales when the new rules go into effect.

Mistaken Extrapolations

The constant temptation in sales forecasting is whether to extrapolate historical sales patterns into the future. While this can be a viable option when sales appear to be following a predictable pattern and the industry is stable, it can be a real concern when this is not the case. When the market is relatively new or subject to disruption, it could be quite dangerous to extrapolate sales data. Extrapolation is particularly dangerous when sales have been spiking for the past few years, but there is a danger that they will peak in the near future; in this case, a business might invest heavily in infrastructure to meet expected demand just when sales flatten.

Characteristics of the Market

Before developing a sales forecast, one should have a firm understanding of the characteristics of the market into which the company is selling. Doing so makes it easier to develop forecasts. For example, do sales tend to be seasonal? If so, what proportion of sales occur in each month? Does this seasonality vary by region? For example, the sale of snow shovels might be quite brief in northern New Mexico, where winter conditions do not last long, but could cover most of the year in Alaska.

Another market characteristic is the size of the market. How big is the total market into which the company is selling, and how much of a market share does the company have? It tends to be quite difficult to expand market share, since competitors will erect stout defenses (such as a price war) to prevent any encroachment.

> **Tip:** It may not be especially difficult to grab a small slice of a market, but it becomes increasingly difficult to pick up larger chunks of the market, since this is the point at which a company will gain the unwelcome attention of competitors. This is why there are many small competitors and very few large ones.

A major point to investigate is the rate at which the market is growing – or not. If the market is only growing at a modest clip, then it will be difficult to justify a large bump in the sales forecast, since the only way to make large gains is by taking market share away from someone else. If the market is declining, then expect recurring price wars among competitors who are trying to maintain their market share. In the latter situation, the sales forecast should probably point in a downward direction – not up.

An essential characteristic of any market is the quality and quantity of the competition. It is especially difficult to gain sales against high-quality competitors who have world-class capabilities in cost control, customer service, product design, and so forth. Another concern is when there are few barriers to competition, so that anyone can enter the market with a minimal investment; in this case, the ongoing expectation should be a swarm of competitors who are desperate for business, and who will reduce prices savagely in order to do so.

A difficult issue to predict, but which still bears examination, is changes in the buying behavior of the firm's customers. Is there a trend away from what customers have historically purchased and towards something entirely different? And if so, how well positioned is the company to take advantage of this change? Or (more likely), can it expect to see a decline in sales because of the change?

EXAMPLE

One of the all-time classic changes in customer buying behavior was the switch from film-based cameras to digital ones, followed almost immediately by the switch from digital cameras to cell phone cameras. The first changeover caused massive declines in film sales at Kodak, while the second switch hammered sales at the pocket-sized digital camera manufacturers, such as Olympus. Neither market has been eliminated – for example, Kodak still produces film, but in vastly lower quantities than had previously been the case.

The imposition or relaxation of government regulations can have a profound impact on a market. When more regulations are imposed, this tends to benefit larger competitors, since they can afford the related compliance costs. Smaller competitors may be driven out of the market entirely. Conversely, the relaxation of regulations may attract new competitors. Given these effects, a large business that already has significant market share should consider increasing its sales forecasts when new regulations are imposed, in the expectation that it will gain business from smaller competitors that leave the market.

EXAMPLE

Following a number of massive fraud cases at public companies, the federal government tightened the restrictions imposed on the auditors of publicly-held firms, including fees charged by the Public Company Accounting Oversight Board. Because of these new regulations and fees, only larger audit firms elected to stay in the business of auditing public companies, which allowed them to raise their rates substantially as competition declined.

Elements of the Forecast

Before delving into the many techniques that can be used to develop a sales forecast, one should understand that a forecast is comprised of three elements. The first forecasting element is the *basic sales forecast*. This element is typically the easiest to predict, being comprised of those sales that recur with predictable regularity. The second forecasting element is the *promotional sales forecast*. Sales included in this forecast are the result of scheduled marketing activities taken to incrementally generate more sales. Examples of these activities are discounts from the retail price and two for-one deals, for which information may be distributed by Internet advertising, billboards, television, and so on. The third forecasting element is *new product sales*; there is obviously no sales history on which to base these forecasts, so the marketing department derives an estimate from the sales of similar products, as well as the marketing efforts it is planning for the various product launches.

Since there may be three elements in a sales forecast, the forecasting team needs to consider whether a separate forecasting technique should be applied to each one in order to arrive at the most accurate outcome.

Drivers of Forecast Accuracy

A reasonably accurate sales forecast needs to detect the following items in a company's sales data and incorporate them into predictions for future periods:

- *Recency*. This emphasizes how much (or little) to factor in recent changes in the data. Thus, a good forecasting technique should allow one to put more emphasis on a recent surge in demand, or the reverse. In other cases, there may be a long-term, steady trend that appears likely to continue, so it might be necessary to ignore recent changes away from the trend.
- *Seasonality*. This is a recurring and predictable pattern in sales over the course of a year. A variation on the concept is the industry business cycle, which spans a number of years. A better forecast incorporates seasonality into its monthly predictions.
- *Trend*. This is the direction in which sales are headed (up or down), as well as the intensity of that direction. It is most commonly characterized as the slope of a line, where the intensity is the angle of the slope. A poor to average forecast model assumes that the existing trend will carry forward into the future at its current intensity level. A better forecast alters the trend, either based on other data, or because it has detected a change in the trend in the historical data.
- *Reversals*. This is a situation in which a seasonal pattern or trend reversed itself at some point in the past. When there is evidence of a prior reversal, the forecast should place a reduced emphasis on trend and seasonality for periods further in the future.

Several of these drivers are shown in the following chart. In addition, historical data contains random fluctuations that are caused by unsystematic short-term events.

Trend, Seasonal, and Cyclical Patterns

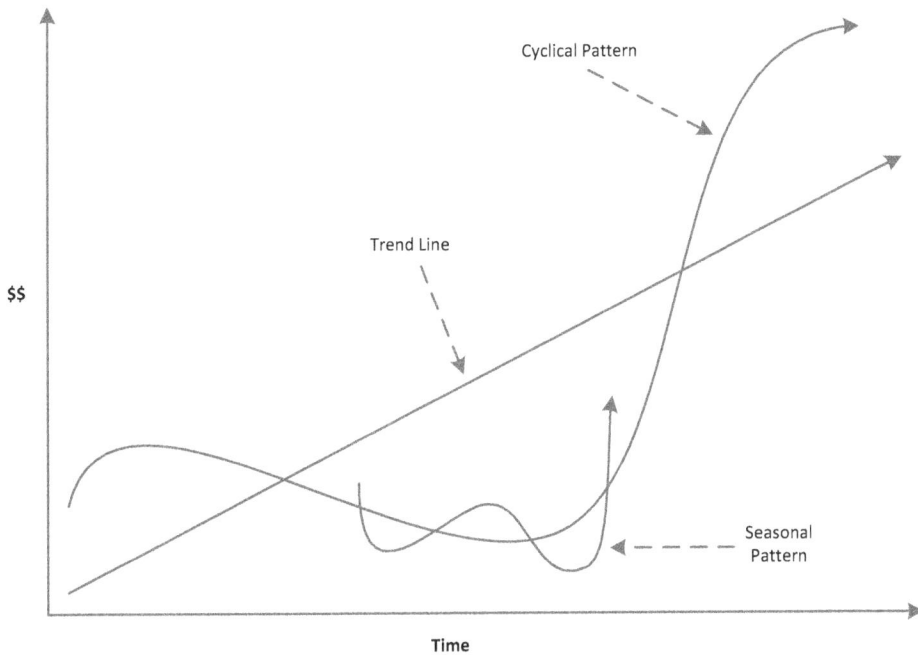

One of the best forecasting techniques that incorporates the preceding drivers is exponential smoothing, which is described later in the book.

An additional factor that the forecaster should watch out for is the *random shock*. This is a sudden change in the level of a firm's historical data, which persists over time. Random shocks are usually not intentional (otherwise they would have a different name). Instead, some type of internal or external event impacts sales, and this influence only gradually dies out. For example, the economy is hit by a pandemic, which results in massive business closures that drive many customers completely out of business. This triggers a sharp decline in the seller's sales figures, which persists for several years while it rebuilds its customer base. These random shocks cannot be ignored if they are still impacting the historical sales data, and may continue to do so into the future.

Sales Forecasting Techniques

In the following sub-sections, we cover many alternative approaches to sales forecasting. As explained in each description, a specific technique is best used only in certain circumstances. So, depending on the complexity of a firm's offerings or the presence of promotional sales or new product sales (as described earlier), it may be necessary to use more than one forecasting method. The following techniques are presented in alphabetical order.

Base Forecast on Changes in Advance Bookings or Orders

Forecasting based on changes in advance bookings or orders is an essential tool in the tourism industry, especially in those areas where travel plans are made months in advance. If advance bookings are down, this likely means that a resort will need to offer cut-rate deals to bring in vacationers at the last minute, which reduces overall revenues. Conversely, an increase in advance bookings may allow a business to increase its last-minute rates for any residual capacity, thereby boosting revenues.

EXAMPLE

The Saba Dive Resort caters entirely to scuba divers, who enjoy the pristine underwater views off the southwest coast of the island. It is now July, and the Caribbean has already been hit by four hurricanes, with additional storms queued up off the coast of Africa and headed towards the Caribbean – and the Saba Dive Resort.

The resort's bookkeeper is attempting to forecast sales for September, when hurricane season will be at its peak. To do so, she reviews the changes in advance bookings for September, and notes that 20% of these bookings have been cancelled, likely due to the nervousness of divers regarding how the hurricane season is trending.

The resort also earns revenue from day-trippers who fly in from St. Maarten with little advance warning. She assumes that the September numbers for this group will drop by an equivalent amount, for the same reason. Her forecast is based on the resort's actual results for the preceding September, which results in the following forecast detail:

	September Actual Preceding Year	September Forecast Current Year
Revenue from advance bookings	$380,000	$304,000
Revenue from day trippers	50,000	40,000
Total Revenue	$430,000	$344,000

Base Forecast on Growth Pattern

A business may release products that follow a predictable pattern of sales growth, flattening, and decline that can be applied to new products. For example, a consumer goods company routinely launches a new product that experiences a three-year growth phase, after which sales level off for five years and then slowly decline – all at predictable rates. When this growth pattern is present, it may be possible to develop a reasonably accurate sales forecast for each new product. This approach works well when a business routinely releases the same type of product.

The main concern with the use of growth patterns is that a new product may not exactly fit the historical pattern, resulting in inaccurate forecasts. To guard against this, one should regularly compare the historical model to actual sales experience and make "on the fly" adjustments to the sales projections based on this latest information. Another option is to initially release the new product in a test market and monitor its sales growth rate to see how closely it matches the company's standard growth pattern; if there is a difference, the modified growth pattern indicated by the test can be applied to this product.

EXAMPLE

Quest Clothiers is a maker of rugged outdoor clothes. It is about to launch an updated version of its expedition kilt (with down insulation). This is a new style for the less-rugged out-doorsman, so the company is uncertain of its reception by consumers. However, a similar kilt style that was released three years ago sold 1,000 units in the first year and then grew at a 10% annual rate for the next two years, after which sales plateaued (as will happen with the fickle kilt crowd). Accordingly, Quest's sales forecast includes a line item for the new kilt that copies the sales experience from the earlier product version.

> **Note:** The essential element of a growth pattern is the *inflection point*, which is the point at which the rate of growth changes significantly. From a forecasting perspective, this means the point at which sales initially start to grow rapidly, as well as the later point at which the rate of growth begins to slow down.

Base Forecast on Leading Indicators

It is sometimes possible to adjust the sales forecast (perhaps substantially) based on leading indicators. A *leading indicator* is a gauge that changes in advance of a new trend in the economic cycle. Examples of leading indicators are the business failure rate, changes in raw material prices, new housing starts, and orders for durable goods. This is a good approach when there is a clear relationship between a specific leading indicator and sales. The use of leading indicators is most warranted when it appears that the end of an uptick or downtick in the economy is approaching.

However, there can be a substantial delay between when there is a change in a leading indicator and when this change is reflected in a company's sales. The delay may be many months, and perhaps longer than a year. Consequently, though leading indicators can be useful, they should be employed with care, perhaps to adjust sales forecasts that have been derived via a different technique.

Base Forecast on Ratios

A business may be driven by a ratio, such as the proportion of customers who make a purchase as a percentage of those who walk in the door (or who access a web site). For example, a web store has 100,000 visitors per month, of which 4% (or 4,000 visitors) make a purchase that averages $100. This works out to $400,000 of revenue per month. Based on this conversion ratio, it is relatively easy to create a sales forecast for future periods. As long as the ratio continues to be valid, the firm can focus on either increasing the number of site visitors per month or increasing the average purchase amount in order to expand its sales.

The ability to forecast based on ratios is predicated on the ability to locate a relevant ratio that can be used to reliably estimate sales, which is not always available.

Consequently, the use of ratios can be limited to certain very specific business types. We have already noted how ratios can be applied to web stores; in addition, the amount of sales per square foot can be applied to retail stores, so that sales are tied to the size and number of retail stores planned for the forecast period.

EXAMPLE

Munchable Donuts currently has 25 stores, averaging 1,200 square feet each. Last year, the company generated $7,500,000 of sales, which was $300,000 per store, or $250 per square foot. In the upcoming year, Munchable plans to open five new stores, all on the first day of the year, and each one with the same square footage. This will result in 36,000 square feet of store space, which at $250 of sales per square foot equals a forecast of $9,000,000.

> **Note:** In the preceding example, we assumed that the five new stores opening on the first day of the forecast year would immediately generate sales at the same amount per square foot that was experienced by the older stores. This is quite unlikely, since older stores tend to generate more foot traffic than new ones. Accordingly, a more precise approach would have been to apply a lower sales amount per square foot to each of the new stores.

Base Forecast on Share of Market

It may be possible to develop an aggregated sales forecast based on a firm's share of the market. This approach can be useful when the market is clearly changing in size, so that sales forecasts are a simple calculation of the market share percentage multiplied by the best estimate of the market size. There are three problems with this approach. First, it can be quite difficult to determine the size of the market, let alone estimate how it will change during the forecast period. Second, one's estimate of a company's share of that market is likely to be imprecise. And third, the company needs to maintain its existing market share percentage through the forecast period, which may not be possible. Given these concerns, it is better to apply the share of market approach to a forecast that has already been derived using some other, more detailed approach, to see if the outcome of the forecast appears to be valid.

EXAMPLE

Erskine's Scotch Eggs Stand is a chain of food shacks in the Canadian maritime provinces that sells Scotch eggs, primarily to those of Scottish ancestry in the area. The Scottish population is growing at a rate of about 2% per year. Based on this growth rate, the company estimates that its sales growth rate will also increase at a rate of about 2% per year – unless it can expand the market to include customers who do not have an ancestral linkage to this decidedly unique food.

Base Forecast on Similar Products

When a business releases a new product, there can be some uncertainty about the sales to be expected from it. One forecasting option is to model the sales of the new product on adjacent products, such as ones with approximately similar features, or which share the same design platform. It may even be possible to develop a forecast based on the estimated sales of competing products released by other companies. This is a reasonable approach when there is sales history available for similar products.

The main failing of forecasting based on similar products lies in the name – these products are *similar*, but they are not the same. Thus, even slight differences in the product price points, features, packaging, and distribution could have a major impact on their eventual sales. An additional concern is that a new product may cannibalize the sales of the products with which it is being compared, so that the sales of the comparison product *decline*. Consequently, the use of comparables is interesting, but is hardly the foundation for an entire sales forecast. Instead, it should be applied only to specific new products for which no other sales information is available.

Base Forecast on Replacement Rate

Customers may be in the habit of replacing their purchases from the company at fixed intervals (such as buying toner cartridges for laser printers). When this is the case, sales for the replacement items can be quite accurately forecasted by multiplying the installed base by a replacement factor (which is derived from historical experience). This is an excellent forecasting approach in situations where customers make repeat purchases.

The main concern with replacement rate forecasts is that this approach only applies to products for which replacements are bought – which may comprise only a small part of a firm's full range of product offerings.

EXAMPLE

An air purifier company sells air purifiers with replacement HEPA filters. At the purchase date, it offers buyers a subscription plan, where it automatically mails them a replacement HEPA filter once every six months. Though some of these deliveries will be rejected, the rejection rate is highly predictable, so the company is able to predict its replacement filter sales with a high degree of accuracy.

Base Forecast on Spending per Customer

Forecasting based on the average spend per customer works well when customers buy a consistent amount per forecasting period. This approach can yield the most consistent results when essential goods are being sold on a repetitive basis, such as food sales by a grocery store. In this scenario, a business probably services customers within a specifically-defined geographic region, who have limited alternative purchasing options. Another example is an agricultural supply store in a farming district where the nearest competing store is 50 miles away.

For more precision in the forecast, it can make sense to stratify customers, since the top and bottom groups of customers may spend substantially different amounts than the median group.

EXAMPLE

Lonely Lake Lodge is the only purveyor of foodstuffs within a 20-mile radius in the backwoods of Minnesota. The owner's customers are comprised of two distinct groups, which are the 500 permanent residents of the area and the 2,000 campers who descend on the area during the summer months. The spending habits of these two groups are entirely different, as outlined by the sales forecast in the following table, which identifies spending by each type of customer for each season of the upcoming year.

	Winter	Spring	Summer	Fall
Full-time residents	480	500	500	480
× Spending/each	$1,200	$1,000	$1,000	$1,200
Full-timer spending	$576,000	$500,000	$500,000	$576,000
Seasonal residents	50	750	2,000	200
× Spending/each	$200	$150	$150	$200
Seasonal spending	$10,000	$112,500	$300,000	$40,000
Grand total spending	$586,000	$612,500	$800,000	$616,000

Conduct a Customer Survey

A sales forecast could be based (at least in part) on a customer survey, asking them about their purchasing intentions. An advantage is that the survey can be administered to a moderate number of customers, from which the results can then be extrapolated. A further advantage is that this approach is relatively inexpensive, and can be administered over a short period of time. In addition, the people conducting these surveys may be able to glean additional information from customers, either through survey forms or follow-up phone contacts, that may provide additional useful information.

However, customers do not always follow through on their stated intentions. When a customer has not already made a deposit on a future purchase, it is all too easy to state a strong intention to buy without having any real reason to do so. Thus, there is a tendency for customer sales projections to be too high. For this reason, it is generally best to use customer surveys as a supplement to other forecasting techniques. If there is a disparity between the outcomes of the techniques, then further investigation may be necessary.

Derive Information from Salespeople

A sales forecast can be based on the projections of the company's salespeople. These people are directly in front of customers every day, and so are in a good position to understand whether they intend to switch away from the company's products or to buy more of its goods and services. They may even be able to provide information about the specific items that each customer plans to buy, and the month in which they will place an order. Salespeople are also on the receiving end of customer complaints, and so have a strong understanding of any product flaws that could interfere with additional customer purchases.

Despite these strong advantages, relying on the sales staff to develop a sales forecast is generally limited to the sale of large-dollar items. This is because salespeople are only employed to sell these items; it is not cost-effective to use sales personnel to sell less expensive goods and services. This characteristic severely limits the use of salespeople for forecasting.

Even in cases where the sales staff is asked for projections, the information they provide may not be entirely accurate, for several reasons. First, they may under-project their forecasts in the expectation of being given lower sales targets for the upcoming year. Second, they do not have a good knowledge of how customers will react to any new goods and services that have not yet been released by the company, and so provide wildly inaccurate forecasts for these items.

EXAMPLE

PropTech manufactures turbines for hydroelectric power plants. Each turbine costs millions of dollars, and the company can also reap millions more in maintenance fees from the decades during which the turbines will remain in service. Given the importance of each order, the company assigns an entire sales team to each customer, which visits the customers regularly. Given the in-depth nature of these sales contacts, the only sales forecasting technique that makes sense is to derive sales numbers from the opinions of salespeople.

Enhance Forecast Based on Price Elasticity

It can be useful to adjust forecasted unit volumes for changes in prices. *Price elasticity* is the degree to which changes in price impact the unit sales of a product or service. Price elasticity is nearly always negative, where an increase in prices leads to a reduction in the number of units sold. This concept is only used as a modifier to an existing sales forecast – it cannot be used as the basis for an entire forecast. Nonetheless, it is an essential consideration when there is a high degree of price elasticity, where a slight shift in prices could have a profound impact on the number of units sold.

EXAMPLE

A personal care product company sells generic plastic combs. Customers base their purchases primarily on price, so a projected price increase of as little as ten cents could result in a 50% decline in the number of units sold.

EXAMPLE

Monique Ponto sells high-end women's watches. Since its products are considered a status item by customers, it has found that modest annual price increases actually *increase* the number of units sold. Apparently, higher prices translate into higher status.

The price elasticity concept should only be applied to a forecast model when there is clear evidence that product sales are sensitive to prices. This can be accomplished by altering product prices in a representative test market and measuring the impact on unit volumes.

Extrapolate Historical Sales Patterns

The most common sales forecasting method is a simple extrapolation of the sales growth rate for the past few years. Extrapolations are a viable option in cases where the market is quite stable, and the business has performed consistently in the market for a number of years. It has the advantage of being inordinately simple to derive in Excel, with the only argument being whether to nudge the forecast up slightly from the historical average or to scale it back somewhat. It also requires no input from anyone, since it can be derived from a spreadsheet analysis of prior period sales. This approach can be used for almost any type of sale, and can at least be applied as a secondary forecasting tool, against which the results of other methods can be compared. And most importantly, the entity has already achieved the prior year sales figure, so there is no question that the required market share exists and that the organization has the capacity to meet the indicated sales level.

In addition to the basic extrapolation of sales figures, the management team can add to or subtract from the prior year actual results for any number of factors that are expected to take place during the forecast period, such as:

- Product price changes
- Additions to production capacity
- Certain customers will be added or dropped
- New sales regions will be added
- New product lines will be added
- New distribution channels will be added

The adjustments to the prior year actuals may be the most difficult to predict, especially if the organization is making changes for which there is no history, such as an entirely new product line.

EXAMPLE

Rubens Trailers specializes in the production of double-wide trailers. Sales of these trailers have proven to be remarkably consistent over the past decade, featuring a modest 2% average growth rate, though demand in the past year came close to maxing out the company's production capacity. For the upcoming year, Rubens has invested in an oversized new production facility that can handle a weighty increase in production.

In the past year, the company had $40 million of sales. The capacity problem will no longer be an issue, so there is an expectation of an additional 2% increase in sales to match the long-term trend, which is $800,000. In addition, the company is launching a standard-width trailer that it hopes will achieve $5 million in sales. Since this is a new product for which there are many competing versions, there is considerable uncertainty about the $5 million figure. Thus, Rubens has a $40.8 million component of its forecast that it considers to be solid, and a $5 million component from which actual results may vary a great deal.

Despite the ease of use of extrapolations, there are also several problems associated with them. A key factor is the derivation of the extrapolation. Who can say whether it should be based on data from the past few years, or maybe just for the past couple of months? Also, should the most recent data be weighted more heavily in the extrapolation than older data? The growth rates resulting from these decisions can be wildly different, so managers must question how the extrapolations were derived. Another concern is that no sales trend lasts forever, so an extrapolated sales increase could prove to be spectacularly wrong when the market reaches its peak and then begins to decline.

A good alternative that has generally proven to be superior to the extrapolation approach is exponential smoothing, which is discussed next.

Use Exponential Smoothing

Exponential smoothing is a forecasting method that is based on historical patterns in the data. It assigns exponentially decreasing weights as the source data gets older. In other words, more recent historical data are given relatively more weight in forecasting than older data. This approach employs a *smoothing constant* in combination with recent and actual forecasted activity to derive a forecast. A smoothing constant determines the level at which actual experience influences a forecast. Thus, if a prior forecast was too high, the smoothing constant is used to reduce the forecast in the next period. Conversely, if a prior forecast was too low, the smoothing constant increases the forecast in the next period. The smoothing constant should be low if the pattern of sales has been relatively stable in the past. The smoothing constant increases in size if there have been large changes in sales. The constant is inserted into the following formula to derive a forecast:

$$\begin{array}{c} \text{New} \\ \text{Forecast} \end{array} = \begin{array}{c} \text{Past} \\ \text{Forecast} \end{array} + \begin{array}{c} \text{Smoothing} \\ \text{Constant} \end{array} \times (\begin{array}{c} \text{Actual} \\ \text{Demand} \end{array} - \begin{array}{c} \text{Past} \\ \text{Forecast} \end{array})$$

The information requirements for exponential smoothing are quite limited. It is only necessary to employ the data from the prior two periods in order to derive the smoothing constant. The calculation of the smoothing constant is as follows:

$$\frac{\text{Period 2 forecast} - \text{Period 1 forecast}}{\text{Period 1 actual demand} - \text{Period 1 forecast}}$$

EXAMPLE

Grizzly Golf Carts uses exponential smoothing in its financial forecasting. In January, Grizzly forecasted that customers would order 300 of its golf carts. Actual demand was 330 carts. The February forecast is that 315 carts will be ordered. The company's forecaster uses this information to derive the smoothing constant, which is calculated as follows:

$$\frac{315 \text{ Carts forecasted in February} - 300 \text{ Carts forecasted in January}}{330 \text{ Carts ordered in January} - 300 \text{ Carts forecasted in January}}$$

$$= 0.5 \text{ Smoothing constant}$$

EXAMPLE

Green Lawn Care forecasted customer orders of 500 electric lawn mowers in the past week, and actual demand for that week was 490 mowers. The company's smoothing constant is 0.2. The company uses the following exponential smoothing calculation to derive the following forecast for the next week:

| New Forecast | = | 500 Units Past Forecast | + | 0.2 Smoothing Constant | × | (| 490 Units Actual Demand | - | 500 Units Past Forecast |) |

$$= 498 \text{ Mowers}$$

In essence, the company is using a modest smoothing constant to slightly reduce its forecast for the next period, since the actual demand in the past week was lower than expected.

Exponential smoothing is among the most popular sales forecasting tools, because it is accurate in a broad range of situations. If it is not possible to develop a usable forecast with exponential smoothing, then it may not be possible to develop a forecast at all with the available data.

Excel provides a tool to generate exponential smoothing forecasts, which is explained later in the Excel Forecasting Tools chapter.

Use Moving Averages

A *moving average* is a calculation to analyze data points by creating a series of averages of different subsets of historical sales data. The best forecasting application for a moving average is when the historical data do not indicate any cyclical or seasonal component to sales. In addition, there should not be an expectation that the forecast will change significantly. When these conditions are present, a moving average is useful for averaging out the irregular components of historical data over a number of periods. The result is a fairly stable forecast. The Excel tool for calculating a moving average is described in the Excel Forecasting Tools chapter.

> **Tip:** Systematically alter the number of periods from which moving average data are taken, and compare the outcome to actual results to determine the optimum number of periods to use for the calculation.

A variation on the concept is the weighted moving average. In this case, the most recent data are considered to be more valuable than older data, so a weighting is assigned to the newer data. An example appears in the following exhibit, where much heavier weightings are given to the immediately preceding two time periods. In the example, a simple average of the three historical periods would have yielded a forecast of $1,000,000. Instead, given the stronger weighting of the final period, the forecast is reduced to $985,000.

Weighted Moving Average Calculation

(000s)	Historical Period 1	Historical Period 2	Historical Period 3	Forecast Period 1
Sales	$1,000	$1,050	$950	---
Weighting points	10	30	60	---
Weighted result	$100	$315	$570	$985

The problem with a weighted moving average is that the weighting is entirely subjective. By comparing the results of a weighted moving average forecast to actual results, one can adjust the weighting to improve the accuracy of the forecast.

An implicit weighted moving average occurs when the number of periods over which an average is calculated is shortened. When this happens, the entire weighting is focused on only the few most recent periods, rather than being spread out over a number of periods. The concept is best explained with the following example. A company is forecasting unit sales using a moving average for the past six weeks. Its calculation for the past six weeks is:

$$\frac{500 + 480 + 540 + 535 + 570 + 585}{6} = 535$$

In this calculation, the weighting is spread evenly over each of the past six weeks. The formula is then changed, so that it only encompasses the past three weeks of unit sales. The formula now changes to:

$$\frac{535 + 570 + 585}{3} \quad = \quad 563$$

In effect, the final three weeks have cumulatively been awarded a 100% weighting, while the preceding three weeks were given a 0% weighting. Consequently, altering the number of periods used in a moving average calculation effectively results in a weighting of the model.

A problem with any type of moving average forecasting system is that detailed records must be kept of the relevant financial information from which forecasts are being calculated.

Use Qualitative Forecasts

A company may choose to adjust its quantitatively-derived forecasts for the opinions of experts in the field. For example, a forecasting team could ask a group of experts to provide their forecasts, from which an average is developed. When using this approach, one should measure the resulting forecast accuracy for the purely quantitative forecast, and separately measure the accuracy of the experts' combined opinion. It is quite possible that the adjustments made by the experts are detracting from the accuracy of the forecast. In addition, consider separately tracking the forecasting accuracy of each expert consulted – some will prove to be more accurate than others.

Use Regression Analysis

Regression analysis is a forecasting method that is based on a cause-and-effect relationship between a dependent and independent variable. The two factors involved in this analysis are:

- *Independent variable*. This is a variable that is not impacted by any other variables being measured.
- *Dependent variable*. This variable is impacted by other variables. An independent variable can cause changes in a dependent variable, but a dependent variable cannot cause changes in an independent variable.

As examples of independent and dependent variables, a person's income (the independent variable) impacts the amount of the individual's spending (the dependent variable). Or, the price of a product (the independent variable) impacts the number of units sold (the dependent variable).

This type of analysis only yields accurate results when the variables used are reliable indicators of an activity. The level of this reliability can be measured using the *correlation coefficient*, for which the formula is:

$$r = \frac{n(\sum xy) - (\sum x)(\sum y)}{\sqrt{[n(\sum x^2) - (\sum x)^2][n(\sum y^2) - (\sum y)^2]}}$$

The symbols in the preceding formula are explained as follows:

x = Independent variable
y = Dependent variable
n = Number of observations

The result of the formula ("r") is a value between negative one and positive one, where a value closer to positive one represents a tight relationship between the dependent and independent variables. The following table illustrates how the output of the correlation coefficient calculation can be interpreted.

Strength of Correlation Coefficient

R Value	Level of Relationship
Positive 0.70 or higher	Very strong positive relationship
Positive 0.40 – 0.69	Strong positive relationship
Positive 0.30 – 0.39	Moderate positive relationship
Positive 0.20 – 0.29	Weak positive relationship
Positive 0.01 – 0.19	Minimal positive relationship
Zero	No relationship
Negative 0.01 – 0.19	Minimal negative relationship
Negative 0.20 – 0.29	Weak negative relationship
Negative 0.30 – 0.39	Moderate negative relationship
Negative 0.40 – 0.69	Strong negative relationship
Negative 0.70 or lower	Very strong negative relationship

Once an independent variable has been found that closely correlates with the dependent variable, a line can be plotted through the data using the following formula for a straight line:

$$Y = a + bx$$

The symbols in the preceding formula are explained as follows:

    Y = Dependent variable
    a = Intercept point of the regression line and the y axis
    b = Slope of the regression line
    x = Independent variable

EXAMPLE

The Sojourn Hotel and Spa has established a strong positive relationship between the number of room guests and the number of spa treatments in the adjacent spa. An analysis of the data results in the following equation that graphs the regression analysis:

$$Y = 100 + 1.55(x)$$

For example, if there are 1,000 room guests in a given period, then the number of spa treatments is estimated to be as follows:

$$Y = 100 + 1.55(1,000)$$

$$= 1,650 \text{ Spa treatments}$$

The calculation indicates that 100 spa treatments are conducted that are not related to room guests, and that each guest pays for an average of 1.55 spa treatments.

An examination of a regression calculation may find that the earlier or later data points used to plot a line result in a closer fit with the line. If so, it can make sense to assign a weighting to the data points, so that those points assigned a higher weighting are factored more heavily into the regression calculation, and those weighted less have a lesser impact on the outcome. For example, a weighting of 1.0 has no impact, while a weighting of 0.7 reduces the impact of a data point, and a weighting of 1.3 increases the impact. The most common application of this concept is to assign a reduced weighting to the oldest data points, so that more recent data are given more weight in the calculation of a fitted line.

The concept of plotting a best-fit line is dealt with in more detail in the Linear Trend Function and Polynomial Trend Function sections in the Excel Forecasting Tools chapter.

A more advanced form of regression analysis is multiple regression analysis, where the impact of two or more independent variables on a dependent variable is analyzed. For example, forecasts could be derived for:

- Sales of Hawaiian helicopter tours that are based on the impact of an advertising campaign *and* the number of visitors to the islands.
- Sales of consumer goods that are based on the impact of advertising frequency *and* the type of media used.

- Sales of freemium products that are based on the price at which the premium product is offered *and* the features offered in the free product.

Tip: Do not attempt to stuff too many independent variables into a regression analysis. When you use lots of variables, some of them will turn out to be highly correlated, which means that some are redundant, and so can be excluded.

A multiple regression analysis should be used when a simple regression does not result in a sufficiently high R value to show a strong relationship between a single independent variable and the dependent variable.

The Regression tool in Excel can be used to obtain information about the relevance of the data used for a multiple regression analysis. See the Regression Analysis section in the Excel Forecasting Tools chapter for more information.

Summary

Clearly, some of these forecasting techniques, such as the weighted average and exponential smoothing methods, can be used as the basis for a comprehensive sales forecast. Other techniques, such as the use of leading indicators, are more ancillary in nature, and so are useful for refining a forecast that was initially derived using other methods. Consequently, a forecaster may need to use a mix of methods to arrive at the most useful forecast.

Tip: From a cost-efficiency perspective, it may not make sense to apply a detailed forecasting analysis to every product being sold. Instead, one could determine which 20% of the company's total product offerings generate 80% of its total sales (known as Pareto analysis), and then focus the most detailed forecasting analysis on just those items.

Detecting Cresting Sales

When a new product is launched, it may initially appear that unit sales will continue in an uninterrupted, steep angle forever. However, the sales of even the most successful product will begin to ebb at some point, either due to increased competition or because the market has become saturated. From a forecasting perspective, the trick is to detect when sales are beginning to crest, so that sales projections in future periods can be brought back down to earth in a reasonable manner. This is a critical task, since a business might otherwise plan for major new investments to support a product line that will soon experience flat or declining sales.

To create a detection system for cresting sales, it is first necessary to recognize the pattern that a business typically follows to keep expanding its total sales. Initial sales begin with a group of core customers at which the product is specifically targeted. Once the rate of sales to this group begins to decline, sales expansion can be pursued using one or more of the following methods:

- Geographic expansion into similar markets, so that the focus remains on the core customers that were originally targeted – they are now located in places that were not initially addressed.
- Price reductions to address more price-conscious customers, possibly with a reconfigured and somewhat lower-cost product.
- Product reconfigurations to address adjacent markets for which the product was not initially designed. This may result in a substantial product redesign, to the point where the revised product would no longer be attractive to one of the original core customers.

The analyst can then segment sales into each of the preceding classifications, and measure the rate of change in sales for each one. The original markets will likely show cresting sales first, as they become saturated. This information can then be extrapolated to the other sales segments, to predict when sales will crest in each successive market.

EXAMPLE

Grunge Motor Sports manufactures dirt bikes, including the Caveman XT, Virile XTO, and Potent 4-Stroke. These machines are specifically designed for the performance-oriented young male. The bikes are sold through distributorships, which the company is slowly opening throughout the country.

Grunge's analyst finds that sales in each distributorship follow roughly the same pattern, which is:

	Sales Growth Rate %
Year 1	40%
Year 2	30%
Year 3	15%
Year 4	2%
Year 5	Flat

This pattern can be applied to each new distributorship in turn to predict when sales will crest.

Grunge then expands its market to introduce a dirt bike targeted at women, called the Petal to the Metal, as well as a dirt bike for middle-aged men, called the Wide Load. These products are positioned outside of the core market group, which results in sales cresting faster – in only three years. This trend is noted in the following table:

	Sales Growth Rate %
Year 1	20%
Year 2	5%
Year 3	Flat

The analyst applies this reduced growth rate to all non-core products. The result of these two sales growth rate patterns is a sales forecasting process that can reasonably predict when sales will crest in each segment of the company's markets.

When there is a suspicion that sales are cresting, it is more important to pay attention to short-term forecasts, since the rate of growth could change over a relatively short period of time. Conversely, it makes much less sense to place an emphasis on long-term forecasts, since they could show sales continuing to rocket skyward. The concept is illustrated in the following exhibit, where a long-term forecast is sufficiently accurate during the spiraling sales period in Year 1, but must be replaced by a series of shorter-term forecasts from Year 2 onward to provide faster notice of changes as the rate of growth declines.

Use of Different Forecasts when Sales are Cresting

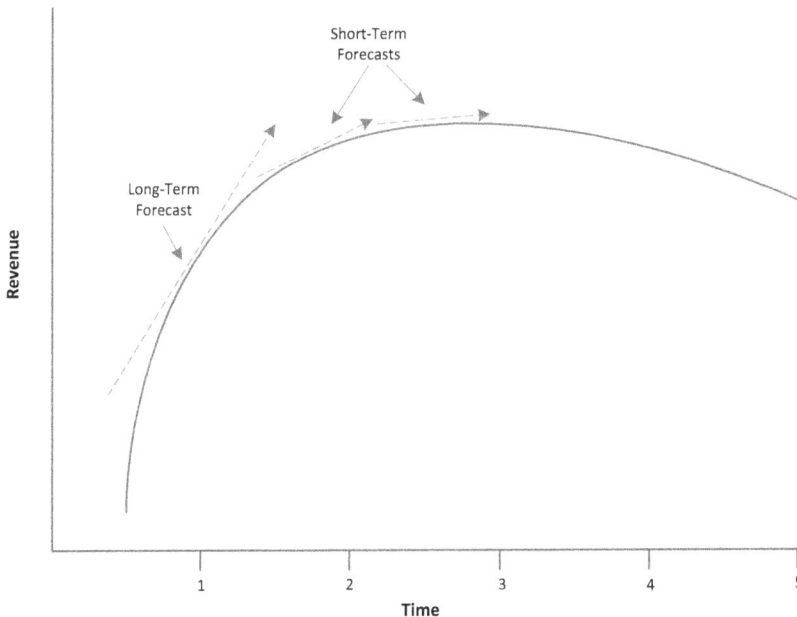

A useful additional concept to consider when monitoring cresting sales is the *saturation level*. This is the point at which all possible buyers have acquired the product or a substitute product, and so will not purchase again, except on a replacement basis. This level can be estimated based on expert opinion and marketing surveys – it is difficult to derive quantitatively without a great deal of expensive investigation. The key point regarding the saturation level is to have an updated estimate of what the saturation level may be, and continually compare this level to actual sales. The comparison is a good indicator of the best case scenario of when sales will crest.

Additional Levels of Forecasting Detail

An additional level of forecasting detail may be needed in some situations to investigate whether projected sales levels can actually be attained. For example, the lowest level of forecasting detail for products is the stock-keeping unit (SKU). At successively higher levels of aggregation, product-related forecasts may be devised for products, product lines, product families, subsidiaries, and entire companies. As another example, the lowest level of forecasting detail for markets is the sales territory. At successively higher levels of aggregation, market-related forecasts can be used for sales districts, sales regions, and entire countries. Alternatively, forecasting detail may be by sales channel, such as direct, retailers, and distributors.

The following exhibit summarizes forecasted sales information by sales territory. This approach is most useful when the primary source of information for the sales forecast is the sales managers of the various territories, and is particularly important if the company is planning to close down or open up new territories; changes at the territory level may be the primary drivers of changes in sales. In the example, the Central Plains sales territory is expected to be launched midway through the forecast year and to contribute modestly to total sales volume by year end.

Sample Sales Forecast by Territory

Territory	Quarter 1	Quarter 2	Quarter 3	Quarter 4	Total
Northeast	$135,000	$141,000	$145,000	$132,000	$553,000
Mid-Atlantic	200,000	210,000	208,000	195,000	813,000
Southeast	400,000	425,000	425,000	395,000	$1,645,000
Central Plains	0	0	100,000	175,000	275,000
Rocky Mountain	225,000	235,000	242,000	230,000	932,000
West Coast	500,000	560,000	585,000	525,000	2,170,000
Totals	$1,460,000	$1,571,000	$1,705,000	$1,652,000	$6,388,000

Another approach is to summarize sales information by contract, as shown in the next exhibit. This is realistically the only viable way to structure the sales forecast in situations where a company is heavily dependent upon a set of contracts that have definite ending dates. In this situation, divide the forecast into existing and projected contracts, with subtotals for each type of contract, in order to separately show firm revenues and less-likely revenues. This type of forecast is commonly used when a company is engaged in services or government work.

Sample Sales Forecast by Contract

Contract	Quarter 1	Quarter 2	Quarter 3	Quarter 4	Total
Existing Contracts:					
Air Force #01327	$175,000	$175,000	$25,000	$--	$375,000
Coast Guard #AC124	460,000	460,000	460,000	25,000	1,405,000
Marines #BG0047	260,000	280,000	280,000	260,000	1,080,000
Subtotal	$895,000	$915,000	$765,000	$285,000	$2,860,000
Projected Contracts:					
Air Force resupply	$--	$--	$150,000	$300,000	$450,000
Army training	--	210,000	600,000	550,000	1,360,000
Marines software	10,000	80,000	80,000	100,000	270,000
Subtotal	$10,000	$290,000	$830,000	$950,000	$2,080,000
Totals	$905,000	$1,205,000	$1,595,000	$1,235,000	$4,940,000

Yet another approach for a company having a large number of products is to aggregate them into product lines and then create a summary-level forecast at the product line level. This approach is shown in the next exhibit. However, if a sales forecast is created for product lines, also consider creating a supporting schedule of projected sales for each of the products within that product line, in order to properly account for the timing and revenue volumes associated with the ongoing introduction of new products and cancellation of old ones. An example of such a supporting schedule is also shown in the following exhibit, itemizing the "Alpha" line item in the product line revenue forecast. Note that this schedule provides detail about the launch of a new product (the Alpha Windmill) and the termination of another product (the Alpha Methane Converter) that are crucial to the formulation of the total revenue figure for the product line.

Sample Sales Forecast by Product Line

Product Line	Quarter 1	Quarter 2	Quarter 3	Quarter 4	Total
Product line alpha	$450,000	$500,000	$625,000	$525,000	$2,100,000
Product line beta	100,000	110,000	150,000	125,000	485,000
Product line charlie	250,000	250,000	300,000	300,000	1,100,000
Product line delta	80,000	60,000	40,000	20,000	200,000
Totals	$880,000	$920,000	$1,115,000	$970,000	$3,885,000

Sample Supporting Schedule for the Sales Forecast by Product Line

	Quarter 1	Quarter 2	Quarter 3	Quarter 4	Total
Alpha product line detail:					
Alpha Flywheel	$25,000	$35,000	$40,000	$20,000	$120,000
Alpha Generator	175,000	225,000	210,000	180,000	790,000
Alpha Windmill	--	--	200,000	250,000	450,000
Alpha Methane Converter	150,000	140,000	25,000	--	315,000
Alpha Nuclear Converter	100,000	100,000	150,000	75,000	425,000
Totals	$450,000	$500,000	$625,000	$525,000	$2,100,000

A danger in constructing a supporting schedule for a product line forecast is that one can delve too deeply into all of the various manifestations of a product (the stock-keeping units), resulting in an inordinately large and detailed schedule. This situation might arise when a product comes in many colors or options. In such cases, engage in as much aggregation at the individual product level as necessary to yield a schedule that is not *excessively* detailed. It is nearly impossible to forecast sales at the level of the color or specific option mix associated with a product, so it makes little sense to create a schedule at that level of detail.

Tip: One thing that very few companies do is to forecast at the customer invoice level. There are so many variables involved at this exceedingly detailed level that it is quite difficult to devise a reliable forecast. Instead, some higher level of data aggregation is needed to generate a forecast.

Advantages and Disadvantages of Forecast Aggregation

It can be quite tempting to only forecast at an aggregated level. Doing so is quite efficient, since there are fewer forecasts to develop, thereby reducing the complexity of the process. For example, by creating a single forecast for a country, rather than for the six sales regions within the country, one can reduce the workload by a factor of six.

Another advantage of aggregation is the increased richness of the amount of data available for use in developing a forecast. For example, someone developing a company-wide forecast would probably be able to rely on a massive data set, whereas someone working on a sales forecast for a specific customer might find that there are no historical sales data at all for long periods of time. Conversely, there might be sharp spikes in the sales data at a very disaggregated level, which are smoothed out when the data are aggregated at a higher level. Thus, it usually makes more sense to forecast SKUs over large parts of a country, rather than at the level of individual sales regions.

There are also some disadvantages associated with forecast aggregation. A key problem is that key local trends or seasonality findings could be lost when forecasts are only viewed at a higher level. This can result in a loss of forecast accuracy. Further, management will not gain the insights into local demand conditions that would have been revealed with lower-level forecasting.

Forecasting Scenarios

A useful aspect of the sales forecasting process is that it forces one to delve into the trends, products, and market forces that underlie sales. Gaining a better understanding of these issues allows for higher-quality predictions.

EXAMPLE

Milagro Corporation produces high-end espresso machines, and projects an 8% increase in its sales in the upcoming year. A pandemic occurs and shuts down many of its restaurant customers. However, sales actually *increase*, as people begin to work from home and want to produce their own espresso there.

This unexpected result causes management to re-evaluate its assumptions about its customer base, and also triggers a product redesign to make it more affordable for home users.

It can be useful for the forecaster to create several distinct models, where each one is designed to address a specific scenario that may impact the company. For example, the sales forecasting process for an airline might generate several outcomes, such as the impact of a pandemic on customer volumes, the impact of jet fuel prices on the prices that must be charged to customers, and the impact of an airplane crash on airplane load percentages.

Summary

When a sales forecasting system is first created, it is quite acceptable to begin with relatively simple forecasting techniques and then gradually increase the level of sophistication of the process. By taking this approach, one can decide upon the most appropriate level of sophistication needed in relation to the cost and time requirements of the process. Also, the procedures used can be gradually enhanced to tighten the amount of time required to complete the process, making it more efficient. This gradual improvement strategy is a good way to arrive at an optimal forecasting system over just a few years.

Chapter 2
The Forecasting Process

Introduction

Sales forecasting is much more than the technical application of a few techniques to a data set. In addition, a team must be assembled to conduct the forecasting that has a specific set of skills. Further, there are a number of constraints that will limit the ability of the organization to generate sales, which the forecasting team needs to factor into its prognostications. And finally, the forecasters need to follow a specific set of processing steps in order to arrive at the highest-quality forecast, which should incorporate a number of best practices. All of these issues are addressed in the following pages.

Sales Forecasting Expertise

A broad set of competencies is required to develop a sales forecast. Ideally, all of the following skills should be present on the forecasting team:

- *Modeling skills.* Given the amount of data collection and modeling required, someone should have a detailed understanding of the available forecasting methods, as well as how to use them within Excel or some other modeling software.
- *Database extraction skills.* Someone should be able to extract historical sales data from the company database, as well as clean up and aggregate the data to put it into a usable form.
- *Communication skills.* Information that can impact the sales forecast is located across the organization, and must be readily accessed by someone who can easily communicate across all levels of the organization.
- *Constraint knowledge.* Someone must have a clear understanding of the bottlenecks within the firm that may interfere with its ability to generate more sales. This may be someone in the production department if there is a manufacturing bottleneck, or someone in the sales department if there are selling concerns, and so forth.
- *Promotions knowledge.* Someone in the sales department who understands the company's marketing campaigns and their impact on sales by period should be able to provide advice about these surges in demand during the forecast period.
- *Trend analysis skills.* Someone should have a firm understanding of developing market trends, seasonality and customer purchase cycles by region, changes in sales channels, and any other factors that may impact the sales forecast.

- *Process management.* In addition to the preceding skills, a manager is needed to coordinate the collection of the data needed to derive a sales forecast, model the data, and process multiple iterations of the forecast, to ensure that it has been properly validated.

Given this broad range of required skills, it is not uncommon to see forecasting teams comprised of members from the sales, marketing, operations, and information technology departments.

In a larger company with many products and sales channels, the forecasting team may be split up into sub-groups that are tasked with forecasting for specific areas. For example, one team might be assigned the sales forecast for a specific sales channel, such as retail stores or Internet sales, while another team is assigned forecasting responsibility by product line or geographic region. There is a clear forecasting overlap among these separate forecasts, so the areas of duplication must be eliminated during a reconciliation process, to ensure that no sub-level forecasts are duplicated in the final sales forecast.

EXAMPLE

Grilled Tofu Company develops forecasts for the sale of its succulent wares not only by individual retail store and by distributor, but also by geographic region. The sales forecasts for each geographic region are compiled separately from the individual retailer and distributor forecasts, based on leading indicators of economic activity and the company's share of the (admittedly small) market for grilled tofu. Given the divergent sources of forecasting information, detail-level and high-level forecasts must be reconciled before a final sales forecast can be issued.

The sales forecasting team is usually organizationally positioned within the sales department. By doing so, the team has ready access to market information obtained from the department's salespeople. However, in cases where sales are mostly on-line, there may not be salespeople from whom to obtain information. In this case, the forecasting team is more likely to be engaged in data analysis supplemented by the planning activities of the marketing department; if so, the organizational positioning of the team is much more open to interpretation.

Another organizational issue is the level of power given to the manager of the forecasting team. This person needs to be at the approximate level of a department manager and be heavily supported by senior management, in order to have sufficient authority to extract forecasting information from the various departments. Since the accuracy of the forecast can be the deciding factor in whether a company earns record profits or suffers humiliating losses, it is critical to give the forecasting manager a great deal of power within the organization.

Constraints Impacting the Sales Forecast

Much of the discussion in this book focuses on the mechanics of the many techniques that can be used to create accurate projections of future sales. However, it is dangerous to focus too much on just the mechanics of this process, for they can be severely impacted by a number of adverse situations. Consider the following possibilities:

- *Salesperson replacements.* If a highly experienced salesperson leaves the company, it is quite likely that a less-skilled replacement will generate fewer sales.
- *Salesperson funding.* If management wants to increase sales next year, is it funding the addition of a sufficient number of salespeople to support that effort? And is it planning to fund a sufficient amount of training for them? Furthermore, is it planning to provide funding for too many salespeople, in the expectation that some will quit or be pushed out due to inadequate performance?
- *Commission changes.* If a new commission plan will go into effect during the budget period, how will it impact the willingness of the sales staff to sell? Alternatively, will the compensation structure of the new plan push the sales staff in the direction of selling different products (which alters the sales mix)?
- *Product cannibalism.* If the company is expecting to launch a new product during the budget period, will the sales of the new product interfere with the sales of an existing product?
- *Competition.* Have any competitors signaled that they plan to issue competing products or engage in other forms of disruptive behavior (such as changes in pricing, customer service, and warranties) that could impact sales?
- *Marketing funding.* Will management give the marketing department the same amount of funding as last year? If not, this will impact the quantity and type of marketing programs conducted, which has a direct impact on the amount of sales brought in. For example, a budget cut forces the marketing manager to entirely eliminate a firm's coupon program, which used to drive about ten percent of total company sales. Some of those sales may still occur, but it is likely that some price-sensitive customers will buy elsewhere.
- *Supply problems.* Are there any indications that supplies of critical components may be constrained? If so, the company's ability to produce certain goods may be limited.
- *Product pricing.* Is management planning to increase prices? If so, some customers will probably depart in search of better pricing, thereby reducing the amount of sales that can be achieved.
- *Product withdrawals.* Do customer complaints indicate that the company may have to withdraw a product from the market? And if so, for what period of time would the product be withdrawn?

> **Tip:** Consider organizing the sales forecast line items by probability and providing subtotals by probability range. Doing so gives a reader a ready grasp of the likelihood that the company will achieve its sales targets. In addition, consider color-coding each probability cluster to make the delineation more obvious. For example, to use a stop light color scheme where high-probability sales are presented in green, all moderate-probability items in yellow, and low-probability sales in red.

A common trap that companies fall into when forecasting for rapid growth is to account for the delaying effect of pacing. *Pacing* is the rate at which an entity can ramp up an operational issue until it can handle a target sales level. Here are several pacing scenarios to consider:

- *Sales staff.* A company sells a product that requires an intensive hands-on sale by an experienced salesperson. The company must delay budgeted revenues that are associated with new salespeople until such time as they are capable of selling at the same success rate as more experienced salespeople. This is one of the most significant pacing issues.
- *Selling cycle.* In some industries, customers only buy products at a certain pace. This is particularly true for large capital products, where purchases are only considered once a year, and must go through a lengthy review process before a purchase order is issued. In such situations, a company may hire a group of excellent, well-trained sales people, and yet not earn a single new customer order for a long time.
- *Retail roll out.* A company has developed an excellent retail concept store, and can gain sales rapidly if it can roll out the concept into new locations as fast as possible. This is a major pacing issue, since the company likely has only a small number of people who are sufficiently skilled in store openings, and that group can only open a certain number of stores within a given period of time.
- *Production facilities.* If a company can only gain new sales after it builds new production facilities, then it cannot forecast more sales until the facilities are complete and tested, and the new staff hired for the facility is capable of running the facility at the planned level of productivity. The variety of issues involved can mean that new sales cannot begin until a long time after a facility has been constructed.
- *Permits.* A company can only do business in a new sales region after it obtains all necessary government permits. This is a particular problem when a company is attempting to gain entry into a new country where it has few contacts or no local partners.
- *New technology.* A company has created a product that has cutting-edge technology. Such products tend to have a higher failure rate until the engineering and production staffs can figure out the underlying issues. This process of working out the kinks can be extensive and greatly delay revenue generation.

Pacing is an important topic that less seasoned managers tend to completely ignore. The result is a sales forecast that initially appears reasonable, but which a company is not able to meet, due to a lack of attention to underlying factors that exert a natural slowing effect on sales growth.

The Forecasting Process

Based on the plethora of forecasting techniques noted earlier in this book, we can derive a standard forecasting process flow. A structured process is quite useful, since it allows for a considerable degree of standardization in forecasting. This has several benefits. First, anyone following the standard process should be able to achieve the same forecasting results, with the exception of some variation relating to personal judgment calls on qualitative forecasting issues. Second, with a regimented system in place, it is easy to tweak the approach to adjust for forecasting errors found in prior periods, thereby making it possible to improve forecast accuracy over time. This means that the process builds on the forecast results achieved in prior years, so that the forecasting process should become more sophisticated over time. Given these advantages of using a standardized forecasting process, we suggest that the following steps be followed:

1. *Conduct research.* Delve into the markets served by the company, in order to understand the size of the market and the firm's share of it. Also learn about the market's rate of growth, based on historical patterns and any applicable leading indicators.
2. *Determine the forecasting mix.* Decide upon the main methods to develop the forecast. It is quite likely that the best mix of methods will begin with a single baseline method (such as historical extrapolations), which is then modified by several other techniques to yield a more refined forecast.
3. *Specify assumptions.* Itemize every key assumption to be used in the forecast, and discuss them with others who are associated with the generation of revenues, to confirm whether the assumptions are valid.
4. *Collect data.* Pull in data from multiple reputable sources, which will then be used in the development of the forecast. It is useful to obtain data from more than one source, and preferably from unrelated sources, to see if the sources support each other. Examples of these sources are trade journals, internal databases, and market surveys.
5. *Authenticate the data.* Ensure that the data are valid. This means reviewing the credibility of the sources and comparing data sets to see if any data appear to be inaccurate.
6. *Plot the data.* It is much easier to spot unusual or unexplained occurrences in the data by constructing a plot. Also, a visual check can reveal many of the drivers of forecast accuracy – the recency, seasonality, and trend of the data, as well as the presence of any trends. The model can then be constructed with this visual observation in mind.
7. *Construct the model.* Develop a forecasting spreadsheet that lays out the elements of the forecast, compiles the forecast by period, and documents all

assumptions. It can be helpful to place all variables in a clearly-delineated part of the forecast, where they can be easily adjusted and compared to the resulting forecast changes. Examples of the variables that may be incorporated into the model are:

- The rate at which prices will decline if competition increases
- The rate at which unit sales will decline if the government caps unit sales
- The price sensitivity of the product
- The rate at which sales should increase for every salesperson added
- The company's presumed market share
- The rate of the growth (or decline) of the market

> **Tip:** Whenever the variables in a forecasting model are adjusted, be sure to record the resulting changes to the forecast. Otherwise, it is tempting to make a number of changes at once, and then not know how each element of this smorgasbord of adjustments impacted the results. At a minimum, keep track of the original settings for the variables, so that you can return to them and start over.

8. *Test the model.* Verify that the model works – which will very likely not be the case in its first few iterations. Make changes to the model's variables and other inputs to verify whether they result in the anticipated changes to the forecast. For example, load in a set of variables that should create a more aggressive forecast, and then do the same for a low-growth scenario.
9. *Validate the outcome.* It is extremely common for a sales forecast to be completely out of touch with the realities faced by a business, even though the underlying model appears to function in an acceptable manner. To keep this from happening, validate the outcome by comparing it to the historical sales of the business, as well as all constraints that it faces, and its ability to support the working capital levels required by the forecast.
10. *Validate organizational capabilities.* An excellent additional step is to walk the forecast through the company, discussing its outcomes with knowledgeable parties to see if they can spot any problems worth rectifying. In particular, operations managers should address whether it is even possible to meet the sales targets outlined in the forecast. It is quite likely that this analysis will call for a reduced forecast that is within the operational capabilities of the organization.
11. *Present the forecast.* A forecast is useless unless it is accepted by management. To improve the odds that this happens, craft a presentation that lays out the key variables incorporated into the model, the constraints limiting the size of the forecast, and the resulting forecast numbers at an aggregate level. The ideal presentation should be restricted to a fairly high level of aggregation, to maintain the attention of the audience.

> **Tip:** Any constraints noted during the meetings to validate organizational capabilities should be fully documented and forwarded to management, noting the impact of these issues on the sales forecast. Management will likely need to address these concerns before the company can expand its sales much further.

Sales Forecasting Structural Improvements

There are a number of structural improvements that the forecasting team can make to the forecasting process in order to achieve higher-quality outcomes. We present several possibilities in the following sub-sections.

Understand the Addressable Market

The first enhancement to the sales forecasting process is simply to gain a better understanding of the addressable market. Doing so makes it easier to evaluate whether it is possible to enhance sales, and how this may be achieved.

There are a number of market issues to learn about. For example, what types of customers does the company serve? Do they have high or low incomes? What do they want from the company? What sorts of praise or complaints are they sending to the customer service department? How many product categories are positioned within the addressable market? How many of these categories is the company filling with its products? What is the range of services offered by the company, versus the offerings of competitors? Should it just sell products, or also offer in-home installation? What about field servicing to fix broken products? Is it possible that competitors are entering the market from adjacent markets? If so, what special advantages do they have? Why are current customers switching to them?

EXAMPLE

A company manufactures small flashlights, which it markets as being emergency use items that are kept in the glove box of one's car or in a closet at home. Its sales are almost completely destroyed when cell phones with integrated lights hit the market. The company had not anticipated that a competitor could come from the cell phone market, which it would not have considered to be an adjacent market.

Clarify Definitions

Whenever more than one person is involved in the sales forecasting process, expect confusion about the meaning of the terms used in the forecast. For example, are you asking people for information about the number of units that will be sold, or the dollar amount that will be sold? Also, when specifying the months in which sales will be achieved, specify the difference between the order placement date and the delivery date (when the sale is most likely to be recognized); there could be a gap of several months between these dates, so make sure that everyone understands the difference.

Clean Up the Data

In the preceding chapter, we noted that unreliable data can be a primary cause of a poor forecast, and pointed out several reasons why such data may arise. It is always best to derive a forecast based on a large amount of data, so if at all possible, try to clean up the data rather than eliminating items that appear to be somewhat questionable. For example, if old sales data were recorded when the underlying accounting standards were different, see if there is a cost-effective way to adjust the old data to comply with the current accounting standards. If it is not cost-effective (or even possible) to clean up the data, then it should be excluded from the formulation of the forecast; however, such a reduction leaves less data for the forecasting model to work with, and so should be considered the last viable option.

A particular concern arises when a company has engaged in one or more acquisitions, so that its historical sales level shows sudden spikes when the sales associated with each acquiree are added to the firm's accounting records. In this case, a possible option is to create a separate forecast for each subsidiary and then combine them into a company-wide forecast. This approach allows the forecasting team to incorporate the drivers of forecast accuracy (recency, reversals, seasonality, and trend) that are unique to each subsidiary. An alternative is to remove all data prior to the date of the company's last acquisition, so that the forecasting technique is only dealing with the combined results of all current subsidiaries; however, this may eliminate a large amount of the historical information that would otherwise be available for forecasting purposes.

Specify All Assumptions

As noted earlier, faulty assumptions can lead to a poor forecast. Accordingly, it makes sense to state in the forecast all assumptions used in its derivation. By putting them front and center, users of the forecast can decide for themselves whether these assumptions are reasonable. Here are several assumptions that might be included:

- We believe that our products remain sufficiently differentiated to justify a 10% price premium over the market price.
- We assume that the northeastern market will continue to grow at a 4% rate, and that the western market will continue to grow at a 10% rate.
- We believe that we can raise prices by 5% and only suffer a 1% unit volume decline as a result.
- We believe that our main base of customers is working mothers.

Assumptions should be included in summary form in the final report sent to management, so that they can evaluate the forecast in light of the associated assumptions.

Address Constraints

There may be a number of constraints, both inside and outside of the company, that will limit any further increases in sales. For example, when a company already has a dominant market share in its chosen market, what are the odds that it can squeeze additional sales from that market? Or, constraints in the production process do not allow the firm to produce more units than it is already manufacturing. In these cases, management needs to be realistic about how it is going to produce additional sales.

Forecast to the Lowest Level of Operational Need

It is much easier to forecast sales at the most aggregated level, since there is only one number to forecast each month ("our sales in January will be $12 million"). Also, the forecast tends to be more accurate at an aggregated level, since forecasting errors for individual SKUs tend to balance each other out when they are added together. However, a highly aggregated forecast probably does not meet the needs of the organization. For example, the purchasing manager needs to know about the exact quantities of raw materials to purchase, which cannot be done unless the forecast is sufficiently detailed to provide her with forecast unit numbers for individual SKUs. As another example, the production manager for a product line needs to know how many units will be run through his machinery in the coming year, which calls for sales forecasting at a fairly detailed level. In short, the sales forecast should be prepared at the level of detail needed by those departments that must act on the information.

Forecast Unit Volume

Forecasting results will generally be better when a forecast is stated in units, rather than dollars. As just noted in the last sub-section, unit-level information is needed for operational planning. At a minimum, ensure that unit volumes are stated somewhere in the forecast.

Forecast Based on Triggering Events

In many industries, forecasts can be quite lumpy from month to month, and not just because of seasonality. Instead, sales may spike due to a new product introduction or decline due to a product withdrawal. Or, a new sales territory may be opening up, or perhaps a cluster of retail stores is being opened in a new geographic region. As another alternative, the business may be starting to receive an entirely new revenue stream, such as royalties from the use of intellectual property. Each of these events should be itemized in the sales forecast, along with the best estimate of a start date for when these events will occur.

Track Forecast Variances Against the Source

Some information sources are better than others. For example, one salesperson's forecasts might prove to be quite accurate, while another's forecasts are consistently too high or low. Similarly, some survey participants might state during the survey that they want to make purchases from the company, and then fail to do so. Given these disparities, it makes sense to monitor the forecast versus actual variance for each information source; when there are significant differences, consider constructing the next forecast without the information sources that have proven to be questionable.

Link Forecast Accuracy to Incentives

The development of a sales forecast should not be an academic exercise to which the forecasting team only has an intellectual connection. Instead, they should be penalized or rewarded, depending on how accurate the forecast turns out to be. This means that the team leader should be responsible for the quality of the forecast as a whole, while individual team members should be responsible for the parts for which they were assigned responsibility (such as a specific product line).

It can be quite difficult to estimate sales by month with precision, whereas the forecasting team may be able to derive reasonably accurate forecast numbers for the entire year. Therefore, it can make sense to assess forecast performance on a cumulative basis as the year progresses, rather than hammering the forecasting team just because (for example) a customer order expected in May did not arrive until the first day of June.

Shorten the Forecast Horizon

In cases where forecast accuracy declines rapidly after a few months, consider cutting off the forecasting horizon at that point, rather than attempting to extend it out for a full year. This is an especially attractive option in nascent markets that are still evolving.

The downside of repeatedly issuing new sales forecasts is the extra time required to generate them. In addition, using a series of short-term forecasts can reduce the credibility of the overall forecasting process, since it may result in a succession of forecasts that differ markedly from each other. Furthermore, it may be difficult to create long-term sales incentive plans when the underlying sales forecast is constantly changing. Nonetheless, a shorter forecasting horizon is recommended in more unstable markets.

A shorter forecasting horizon is quite useful when dealing with new products and services, and especially when they are located in entirely new markets. In these cases, there is a high probability that the initial forecast will vary substantially from actual results, so a string of forecast revisions within a short period of time will likely be needed, until the company gains some actual sales data in this area.

A follow-on question to the concept of shortening the forecast horizon is how short can it realistically be made. The answer is driven by the operations of the business. That is, the forecast should encompass the lead times of its supply chain. For example, if a clothing company outsources its production to Vietnam and the goods are shipped by ocean freight back to it, then the time interval from when it places an order with the supplier to when it receives the order may be a couple of months. Therefore, it must be able to forecast sales for that period of time or longer; otherwise, it will have no basis upon which to place orders with its suppliers.

A Note on Performance Measurement

When sales forecasts are created and then made the responsibility of various people within the hierarchy of the sales department, an interesting performance measurement issue arises. The vice president of sales is most likely to come closest to making his or her assigned sales goal, while the percentage variance will tend to increase as responsibility is shifted lower down in the hierarchy, from the district managers to the individual sales people. This condition is caused by the law of large numbers, which states that as a sample size grows, its mean gets closer to the average of the whole population. For example, if you were to flip a coin many times, the number of times that heads or tails come up should be almost the same. However, if you were to flip the coin just a few times, there might end up being an inordinate number of one side or the other occurring. Thus, there may only be a modest number of sales to customers in a given month within a small sales region, while there could be hundreds of thousands of sales transactions across the entire company.

What is the impact of the law of large numbers on the employees of the sales department? There could be a high degree of variability in the sales results of individual salespeople from month to month (unless they manage it by deliberately accelerating or deferring some customer orders), so that they find it quite easy to attain their targets in some months and nearly impossible in others. Meanwhile, the sales results for which the vice president of sales is responsible will be far less variable, so that actual results are more likely to trend relatively close to the sales forecast in every month. This condition might be worth remembering when constructing performance compensation plans for those salespeople at the bottom of the departmental hierarchy. This high degree of variability for salespeople could result in some of them being fired because they are performing well below a quota that may be too high, while others easily earn bonuses on quotas that are too low.

Summary

A sales forecast is only as good as the quality of the assumptions, variables, and other inputs from which it was constructed. Consequently, the research and decisions made as part of the modeling process are essential to the quality of the forecast output – and these efforts are based on the range of skills of the forecasting team. To ensure that this team consistently constructs high-quality forecasts, it should follow a standard process, working through each task thoroughly to ensure that every assumption, data source, forecasting model and so forth has been fully explored. Even then, the resulting model's projections should be tested against the constraints faced by the business. This type of careful analysis is needed to derive reasonable forecasts that a business is actually capable of attaining.

Chapter 3
Excel Forecasting Tools

Introduction

The Microsoft Excel electronic spreadsheet contains a number of tools that are useful for sales forecasting. They include the automated calculation of moving averages and exponential smoothing, and the creation of trend lines that are based on historical data. Some of these tools are available as standard features of Excel, while a few require that the Analysis Toolpak be downloaded. In the latter case, we provide instructions for how to complete the download. In the following sections, we describe the uses to which these Excel functions can be put, and provide instructions on how to use them.

Moving Averages Function

A moving average calculation generates a sales forecast based on the most recent historical information. Excel provides a tool that automatically creates a moving average from this data. To use the moving averages function, it is first necessary to download the function into Excel. To do so, select the **File** tab, then **Options**, and then **Add-Ins**. Select the **Analysis Toolpak** to download the analysis functionality into Excel. Once the Toolpak is loaded, follow these steps:

1. Enter on an Excel spreadsheet a series of data points relating to the information to be forecasted. A sample appears below.

	A	B	C
1			
2		Period	Unit Sales
3		1	17,400
4		2	16,900
5		3	17,900
6		4	17,400
7		5	18,300
8		6	16,400
9		7	18,500
10		8	17,700

2. Select the **Data** tab and pick the **Data Analysis** option. When the following **Data Analysis** box appears, select the **Moving Average** option and click on **OK**.

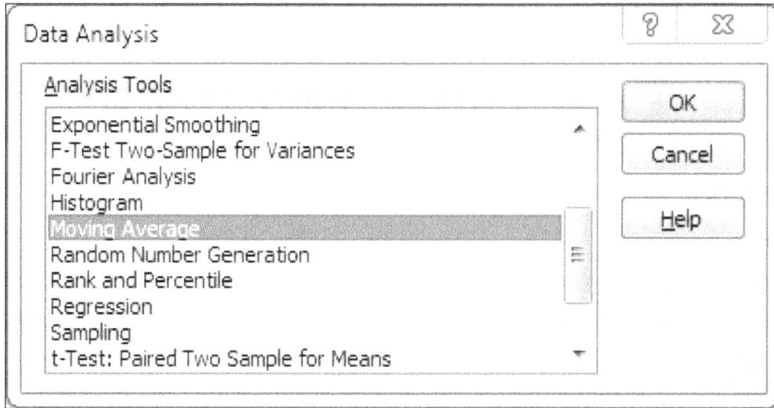

3. The following **Moving Average** box appears. Enter the cell input range (in this case, cells C2 through C10) in the **Input Range**. Enter the cell address range for the resulting moving average (in this case, cells D3 through D10) in the **Output Range**. The completed Moving Average box follows.

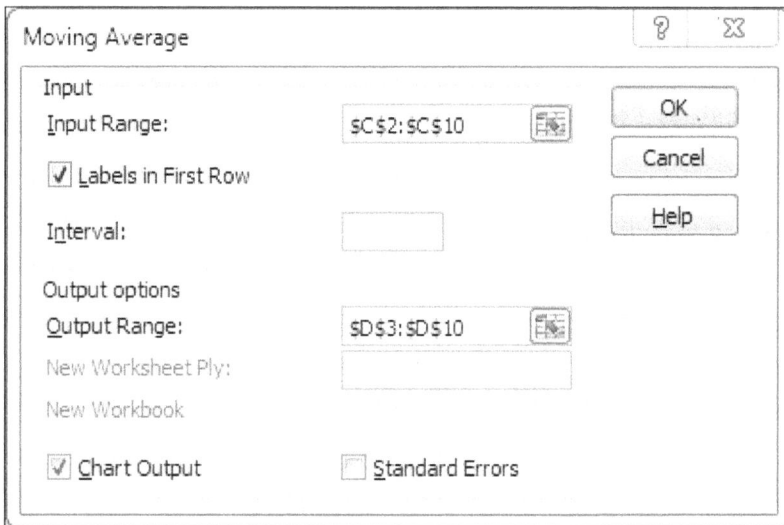

4. Excel automatically creates a moving average based on the listed data, which appears in column D in the following page view, along with a moving average chart. The chart was triggered because we checked the **Chart Output** option in the preceding **Moving Average** box.

	A	B	C	D	E	F	G	H	I	J
1										
2		Period	Unit Sales							
3		1	17,400	#N/A						
4		2	16,900	#N/A						
5		3	17,900	17,400						
6		4	17,400	17,400						
7		5	18,300	17,867						
8		6	16,400	17,367						
9		7	18,500	17,733						
10		8	17,700	17,533						
11										
12										

Moving Average chart showing Actual and Forecast lines, with Value axis (15,000 to 19,000) and Data Point axis (1 to 8).

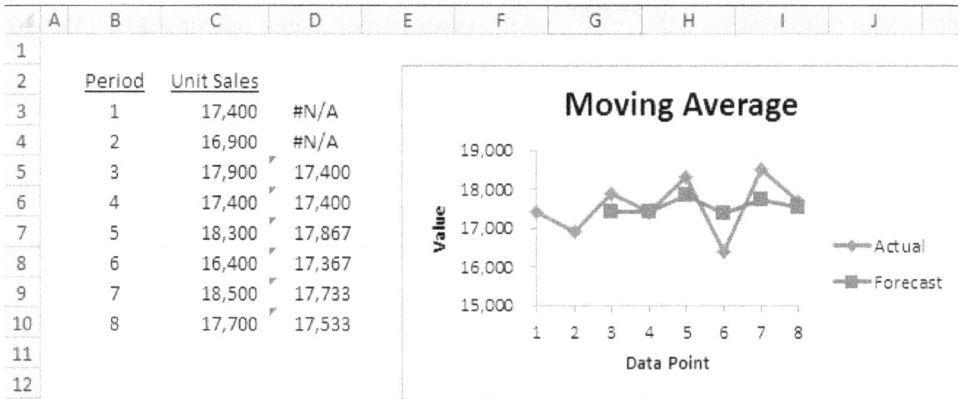

Exponential Smoothing Function

Exponential smoothing is a variation on the preceding moving average concept, where the key difference is the presence of a damping factor in the options that Excel presents. The damping factor is 1 minus the smoothing constant. The *smoothing constant* determines the level at which actual experience influences a sales forecast. Thus, if a prior forecast was too high, the smoothing constant is used to reduce the forecast in the next period. Conversely, if a prior forecast was too low, the smoothing constant increases the forecast in the next period. A high damping factor smooths out the peaks and valleys in the data more than a low damping factor.

To use exponential smoothing in Excel, follow the same steps just noted for the moving average function, except you should select the **Exponential Smoothing** option when the **Data Analysis** box appears. Completing the box while using the same data points just noted for the moving average example results in the following entry in the **Exponential Smoothing** box:

Exponential Smoothing

Input
Input Range: $C$2:$C$10
Damping factor: 0.9
☑ Labels

Output options
Output Range: $D$3:$D$10
New Worksheet Ply:
New Workbook
☑ Chart Output   ☐ Standard Errors

OK   Cancel   Help

The result of this entry is the following exponential smoothing outcome generated by Excel. Note how the forecast line in the chart is much smoother than was the case with the moving average outcome. This is because the damping factor was set at a high 0.9.

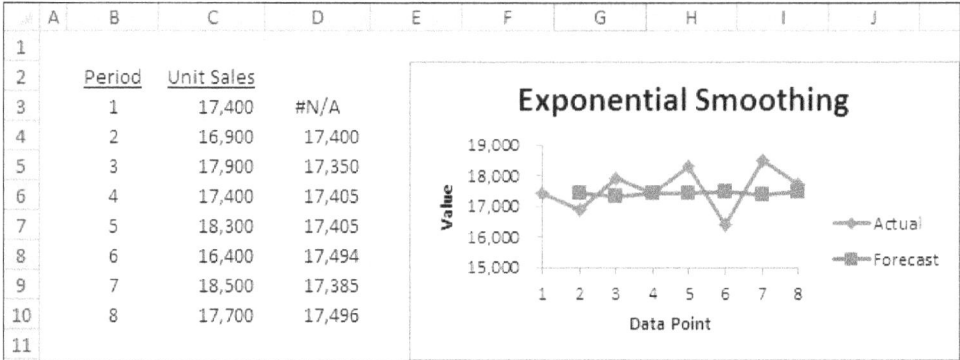

	A	B	C	D	E	F	G	H	I	J
1										
2		Period	Unit Sales							
3		1	17,400	#N/A						
4		2	16,900	17,400						
5		3	17,900	17,350						
6		4	17,400	17,405						
7		5	18,300	17,405						
8		6	16,400	17,494						
9		7	18,500	17,385						
10		8	17,700	17,496						
11										

Exponential Smoothing chart (damping factor 0.9), Value vs Data Point, with Actual and Forecast series.

If the damping factor had instead been set at a much lower 0.1, the outcome would have been as follows, where the smoothing follows the historical data much more closely.

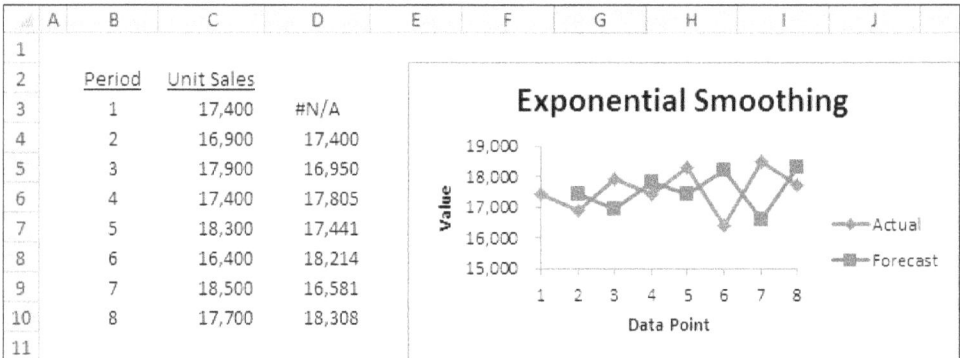

	A	B	C	D	E	F	G	H	I	J
1										
2		Period	Unit Sales							
3		1	17,400	#N/A						
4		2	16,900	17,400						
5		3	17,900	16,950						
6		4	17,400	17,805						
7		5	18,300	17,441						
8		6	16,400	18,214						
9		7	18,500	16,581						
10		8	17,700	18,308						
11										

Exponential Smoothing chart (damping factor 0.1), Value vs Data Point, with Actual and Forecast series.

Linear Trend Function

The linear trend function allows one to highlight a set of consecutive numbers and then drag over additional cells. By doing so, Excel automatically calculates the trend associated with the highlighted numbers and extends the trend line into the additional cells. In the following example, the first three (shaded) cells were originally input into a financial model, and then extended with the linear trend function to create the trend appearing in the next three cells.

Trend Line Calculation

Historical Period 1	Historical Period 2	Historical Period 3	Projected Period 1	Projected Period 2	Projected Period 3
5,000	6,200	7,000	8,067	9,067	10,067

The problem with this dragging function is that the linear trend calculation is not repeated if there is a change in the original data set. Consequently, the drag function is not recommended for high-usage models for which there are expected to be a number of iterations.

An alternative approach is to create a table of all relevant historical values in Excel, plot this information in an Excel chart, and then add a trend line to the chart. The trend line is obtained by right-clicking on the historical data line appearing in the chart and then selecting the "Linear" option. For example, the following time series of data is entered into Excel:

$$3000, 4500, 3800, 5000, 4300, 6100$$

The resulting chart is presented in the following exhibit, along with the associated trend line. Also note that Excel has provided the formula for the resulting trend line within the chart, which is:

$$Y = 460x + 2840$$

The chart also notes that the data has an R value of 0.6642. As noted in the R Value table in Chapter 1, the 0.6642 value indicates a strong positive relationship between the data and the trend line.

Sample Plot of Historical Data with Linear Trend Overlay

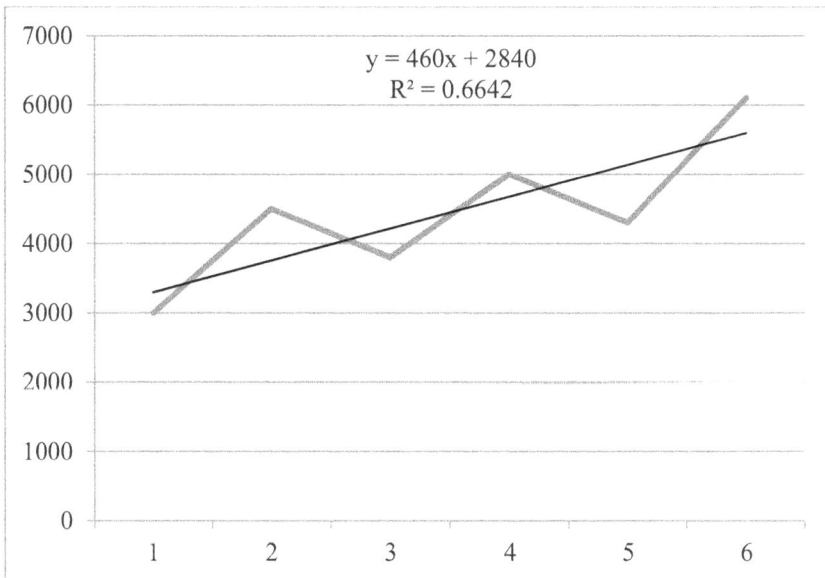

The R value stated in the preceding chart can be a value between negative one and positive one, where a value closer to positive one represents a tight relationship between the dependent and independent variables[1].

Note: A huge problem with the linear trend function is its basis on the assumption that the historical trend is the only relevant sales pattern. It also assumes that the slope of the trend remains unchanged through the forecast period. It ignores seasonality, as well as any changes in the slope of the historical trend. Thus, simply plotting a "best fit" line through a mass of data will not result in the best forecast, but rather a substantial amount of forecasting error.

Polynomial Trend Function

A variation on the preceding linear trend function is the polynomial trend, where Excel fits a curved line to the data. This is especially useful when the data presents either an increasing or decreasing pattern. In particular, it can be used to project an accelerating rate of growth or decline in a sales forecast.

EXAMPLE

The Close Call Company's financial analyst is examining the relationship between the organization's investment in fast delivery trucks in a given geographic region and its ability to make deliveries within one hour. The one-hour deadline is critical to the company, since it earns an automatic bonus from its customers if it makes the deadline.

An examination of the truck investment finds that a small investment has little impact on the ability of the company to achieve bonuses, since there are too few trucks available to drive to pick up locations and from there to drop off locations. The average transit time is simply too long. At a mid-range level of investment, the company maximizes its bonuses. However, when an area is saturated with trucks, the level of bonus achievement only increases at a minor rate, since only the most distant locations in the region can no longer be reached within the required time limit.

Given this relationship between bonus revenue and truck investment, a polynomial trend line would be the best way to fit a line to the data.

As was the case for the Excel linear trend function, relevant historical values can be entered into Excel and then converted into a chart. The trend line is obtained by right-clicking on the historical data line appearing in the chart and then selecting the "Polynomial" option. For example, the following time series of data is entered into Excel:

2500, 3800, 4500, 4750, 4600, 4400

---

[1] A dependent variable is impacted by other variables, while an independent variable is a variable that is not impacted by any other variables being measured.

The resulting chart is presented in the following exhibit, along with the associated trend line. Also note that Excel has listed an R value of 0.9863, which indicates a near-perfect fit between the data and the trend line.

Sample Plot of Historical Data with Polynomial Trend Overlay

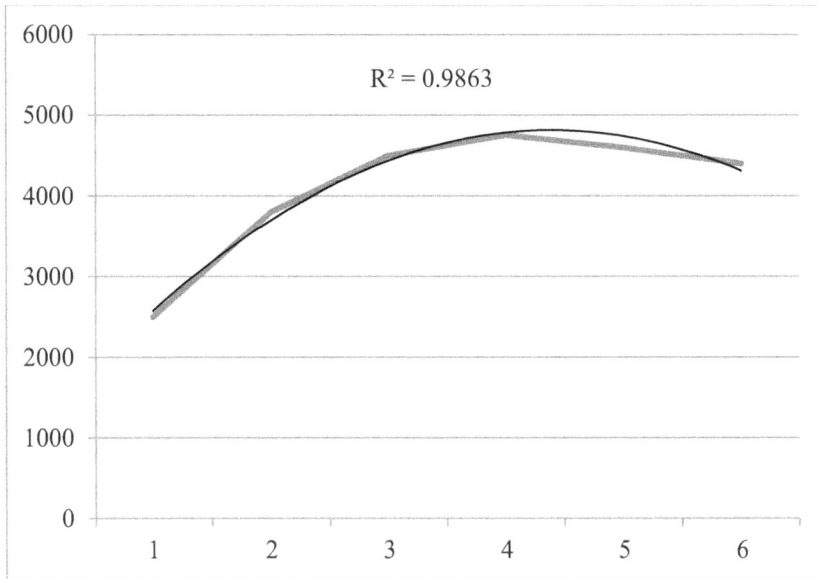

Regression Analysis

The preceding linear trend and polynomial trend functions are adequate and efficient tools for calculating a sales forecast line based on historical data. To gain additional information about the data, the Regression tool is available in Excel.

The regression tool is not immediately available in Excel. To download it, select the **File** tab, then **Options**, and then **Add-Ins**. Select the **Analysis Toolpak** to download the analysis functionality into Excel. Once the Toolpak is loaded, follow these steps:

1. Create a data set that itemizes independent and dependent variables for multiple periods. The following table is an example of such a data set, where we have listed sales (the dependent variable) in the first column, along with the product price and advertising expenditures (independent variables) in the next two columns. We want to see if there is a relationship between the number of units sold and a combination of prices and advertising expenditures.

	A	B	C	D	E
1					
2		Period	Units Sold	Price	Advertising
3		1	4,250	$ 4	$ 5,600
4		2	2,350	$ 10	$ 400
5		3	2,800	$ 6	$ 800
6		4	3,700	$ 4	$ 1,000
7		5	3,100	$ 10	$ 6,400
8		6	3,650	$ 6	$ 3,600
9		7	2,800	$ 4	$ 1,800
10		8	3,250	$ 5	$ 2,800

2. Select the **Data** tab and pick the **Data Analysis** option. When the following **Data Analysis** box appears, select the **Regression** option and click on **OK**.

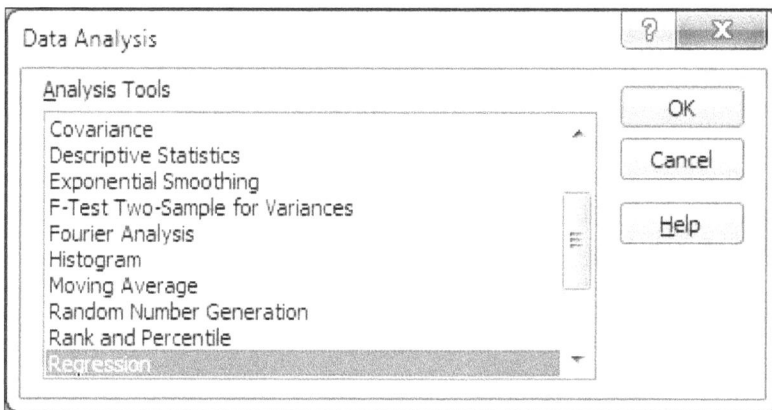

Data Analysis

Analysis Tools

- Covariance
- Descriptive Statistics
- Exponential Smoothing
- F-Test Two-Sample for Variances
- Fourier Analysis
- Histogram
- Moving Average
- Random Number Generation
- Rank and Percentile
- Regression

OK   Cancel   Help

3. The following **Regression** box appears. Enter the cell address range of the dependent variable (in this case, units sold) in the **Input Y Range**. Enter the cell address range of the independent variables (in this case, price and advertising) in the **Input X Range**. Also, select a cell in which the output information will be stated (in this case, just below the data table). The completed **Regression** box follows.

4. Excel automatically creates the following output table. Explanations of the items listed in the table are as follows:

- *Multiple R.* This is the correlation coefficient between the observed and predicted values. It ranges in value from 0 to 1. A small value indicates that there is little or no linear relationship between the dependent variable and the independent variables. The reported 0.846 indicates the likely presence of a linear relationship.

- *R square.* This is the degree of fit between the line generated from the regression analysis and the source data, which is how well the independent variables explain the dependent variable. The 0.717 value in the table indicates a good fit.

- *Adjusted R square.* This value compares the explanatory power of regression models that contain different numbers of predictors – in this case, there are two predictors, price and advertising. The value gives the percentage of variation explained by only those independent variables that in reality affect the dependent variable. The 0.604 value in the table still indicates a good fit.

- *Standard error.* This value measures the accuracy with which a sample represents a population. This is the standard deviation from the mean of the population.

- *Observations*. This is the number of instances of data that were examined to derive the reported results.

12	SUMMARY OUTPUT	
13		
14	*Regression Statistics*	
15	Multiple R	0.846916425
16	R Square	0.717267431
17	Adjusted R Square	0.604174403
18	Standard Error	383.3409096
19	Observations	8

A number of additional analyses are also reported by this regression tool.

Summary

A number of the Excel functions described in this chapter require that data be entered in certain cells in a spreadsheet in a precise manner. This makes the process of setting up an automated sales forecasting function relatively inefficient and error-prone. Consequently, many of these functions are less useful for short-term "one off" forecasting needs. A better use is to incorporate them into forecasting models that are expected to be used on a repetitive basis for a long period of time.

The Linear Trend and Polynomial Trend functions are among the easiest of the Excel forecasting tools, being able to produce useful trend lines and formulas within a short period of time. These functions are recommended for short-term analysis purposes.

Chapter 4
Forecast Evaluation

Introduction

A key task in sales forecasting is managing errors. Some element of every forecast is bound to be wrong, so one should measure the extent of these errors. With that information in hand, the forecasting team can decide whether it is necessary to adjust data sources or forecasting techniques to arrive at a more precise sales forecast. In this chapter, we cover the measurement of forecasting effectiveness, and how this information should be used in the ongoing adjustment of forecasting models.

Measuring Forecast Effectiveness

Monitoring the effectiveness of a forecasting method is a two-step process. First, subtract the forecasted amount from the actual amount, which results in a forecasting error. The following table shows how the forecasting error is calculated.

Forecasting Error Calculation

Period	Forecast Sales	Actual Sales	Forecasting Error
1	$390,000	$430,000	-$40,000
2	450,000	410,000	+40,000
3	420,000	425,000	-5,000
4	465,000	430,000	+35,000
5	440,000	455,000	-15,000
6	470,000	485,000	-15,000
7	500,000	450,000	+50,000
8	510,000	440,000	+70,000
9	490,000	435,000	+55,000

The second step is to plot the forecasting error on a chart, to determine when there is a trend of errors bumping up against or breaking through the maximum acceptable upper or lower error limit. A single spike or drop that breaches a maximum or minimum limit might not be cause for alarm, but a continuing trend of breaches in the same direction may be a sufficient reason to search for an alternative forecasting method. A sample trend error chart follows. In the sample chart, the error rate has breached the maximum threshold for the last three periods, which indicates that the underlying forecast model is no longer a reliable indicator of actual activity.

Trend Error Chart with Min/Max Threshold Levels

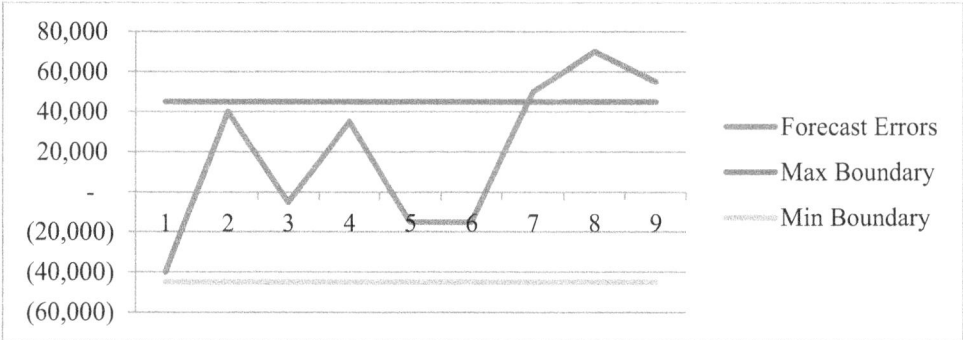

A different type of forecast effectiveness to watch for is the *turning point error*. This is when a forecast does not correctly predict when a trend will reverse. This issue can be critical when production capacity is near its maximum usage level, and any further increases in sales will require a substantial asset investment to support. In such a situation, management needs to know when sales are cresting and will subsequently decline. See the earlier Detecting Cresting Sales discussion for more information.

Another way of looking at the forecast results is to calculate the amount by which, on average, the forecast was either above or below the actual results. Doing so may indicate a bias built into the forecasting methodology that may require correction. For example, during the months when the preceding forecast was too high, the excess forecast averaged $36,000 in five periods. Conversely, during the months when the forecast was too low, the forecast shortfall averaged $18,750 in four periods. Thus, it appears that the forecasting process has a bias in favor of producing overly optimistic outcomes. When a forecasting bias appears to be present, it can make sense to drill down into increasing level of forecast detail to see if there is a particular part of the forecast in which the bias is originating, in order the fix the issue. It is quite possible that the bias is associated with a particular person whose projections are being used in the forecast.

Yet another way of looking at the forecasting error is to strip out the minus signs from the calculated errors, so that all errors are positive values. If this is not done, then the negative and positive values tend to offset each other. By using these absolute values, the forecasting error noted in the prior example results in a significantly different average error – as noted in the following exhibit. In short, by converting the forecasting error to an absolute number for each forecasting period, the average forecasting error in the example is more than $36,000 – as opposed to the prior average error of about $19,000.

Calculation of Absolute Forecasting Error

Period	Forecast Sales	Actual Sales	Forecasting Error	Absolute Error
1	$390,000	$430,000	-$40,000	$40,000
2	450,000	410,000	+40,000	40,000
3	420,000	425,000	-5,000	5,000
4	465,000	430,000	+35,000	35,000
5	440,000	455,000	-15,000	15,000
6	470,000	485,000	-15,000	15,000
7	500,000	450,000	+50,000	50,000
8	510,000	440,000	+70,000	70,000
9	490,000	435,000	+55,000	55,000
Average			$19,444	$36,111

> **Tip:** An interesting alternative to the measurement of forecast errors is to give a larger weighting to the accuracy of forecasts associated with products that have the greatest impact on company profits. The increased weighting calls more attention to forecasting errors relating to high-margin products, as well as to those for which there is a high cost (such as having to make raw material purchases in bulk).

EXAMPLE

Mule Corporation produces two variations on its "Bad Ass" motorcycle. Its Donkey XT model generates a profit of $1,000 per bike, while its classic Ornery XTO model generates twice the profit. Accordingly, management wants to give a double weighting to any variances associated with the sales forecast for the Ornery XTO. In the past year, this resulted in the following variance calculation:

Product	Forecast Variance	Weighting Factor	Weighted Variance	Percent of Total
Donkey XT	$120,000	1.0	$120,000	37.5%
Ornery XTO	100,000	2.0	200,000	62.5%
Totals	$220,000		$320,000	100.0%

A forecast method may have been reviewed, and the conclusion is that it is not effective. Before replacing the method, it may be useful to examine whether other factors are causing the method to produce incorrect results. For example, are the source data sufficiently reliable? It may not be reliable if data are subsequently altered. Also, if there are several sources for the same type of data, do the data vary by source? If so, plug the data from different sources into the forecasting method, and see if the data from one source results in a better forecasting outcome. Finally, is the company using the most recent data? If not, arrange for access to the most recent data, and see if this alters the accuracy of the forecast. If these steps do not improve the forecasting method, it is time to search for an alternative.

Error Correction Logic

At what point should a forecasting team decide to adjust its existing forecasting system? A simple logic flow is to begin with a forecast that is based on a straight extrapolation of historical sales data, and then measure the forecast error. Since an extrapolation is the least sophisticated method, it should have the largest forecasting error. Then work through a series of forecasting enhancements, measuring the forecasting error each time. Whichever technique results in the smallest forecasting error wins. Any forecast that results in an error even larger than the one resulting from an extrapolation of sales data should be ditched.

This error correction logic does not have to be used just on a go-forward basis. On the contrary, it can be used to develop forecasts based on historical data. For example, the forecasting team could use the data available from one year ago in order to forecast sales for the fiscal year that has just been completed, using a variety of forecasting methods. The technique that results in the lowest forecasting error wins, and can then be used to generate a forecast for the upcoming time periods. A major advantage of this historical testing approach is that the forecasting team can engage in rigorous testing before rolling out a new technique, thereby saving the company money through the avoidance of any losses caused by a poor forecast.

Summary

The measurement of forecast effectiveness is one of the most important parts of the sales forecasting process. This represents an iterative loop, where the forecasting team is constantly reviewing its product (the forecast) against actual results, and tinkering with its entire process in order to arrive at a better outcome. In short, only through the constant measurement of forecast errors and subsequent modeling revisions can a business optimize its forecasting outcomes.

Glossary

C

Correlation coefficient. The relationship between an independent and dependent variable.

Cyclical pattern. Long-term movements around the trend line that occur over periods of more than one year.

D

Dependent variable. A variable that is impacted by other variables being measured.

F

Forecasting. The prediction of future events.

H

Holding costs. The costs incurred to store inventory.

I

Independent variable. A variable that is not impacted by any other variables being measured.

L

Leading indicator. Something that can be used to predict future behavior.

M

Moving average. An average of information derived from the most recent time periods in a data set. The oldest values in the data set are dropped from the average as the data from new time periods are added.

P

Pacing. The rate at which operations can be ramped up.

Price elasticity. The degree to which changes in price impact the unit sales of a product or service.

R

R square. A measure of the degree of fit between the line generated by a regression analysis and the source data.

Random shock. A sudden change in the level of a firm's historical data, which persists over time.

Recency. How much to factor recent changes in the data into a forecast.

Regression analysis. A forecasting method that is based on a cause-and-effect relationship between a dependent and independent variable.

Reversal. A situation in which a seasonal pattern or trend reversed itself at some point in the past.

S

Seasonality. A recurring and predictable pattern in sales over the course of a year.

Smoothing constant. A value that determines the level at which actual experience influences a forecast; used in exponential smoothing.

Stock-keeping unit. A specific type of product, with attributes that distinguish it from other SKUs. These attributes may include different sizing, materials, color, and packaging.

T

Trend. A long-term projection of increases or decreases in activity levels contained within the historical information.

Turning point error. The failure to predict when a trend will reverse.

Index

www.ingramcontent.com/pod-product-compliance
Lightning Source LLC
Chambersburg PA
CBHW080721220326
41520CB00056B/7342